SURFACE TRANSPORT FOR RURAL DEVELOPMENT

SURFACE TRANSPORT FOR RURAL DEVELOPMENT

Edited by

Dr. Rabi Narayana Misra

DISCOVERY PUBLISHING HOUSE PVT. LTD.
NEW DELHI-110 002

First Published-2008

ISBN 978-81-8356-259-1

Published by:

DISCOVERY PUBLISHING HOUSE PVT. LTD.
4831/24, Ansari Road, Prahlad Street,
Darya Ganj, New Delhi-110002 (India)
Phone: 23279245 • Fax: 91-11-23253475
E-mail: dphbooks@rediffmail.com
dphtemp@indiatimes.com

Printed at:
Arora Enterprises
Laxmi Nagar, Delhi–110 092

Preface

For economic growth of a country infrastructure plays a vital role in present era. Agriculture and Industry cannot grow itself unless a good infrastructure is available for them. Out of the various infrastructural facilities surface transport claims high priority. Surface transport not only helps for the agricultural development of the country, but also helps for the development of small industries as well as service sector. It is no denying the fact that for the development of rural economy of the country, roads are considered as the most basic need. In absence of adequate rail linkage to rural areas, roads are the major means of transportation in the state of Orissa as well as the country. The surface communication has direct bearing on the quality of the lives of the people. The effectiveness of surface system will help manage the administrative system of the state as well as the country.

Dr. Rabi Narayana Misra

Acknowledgement

I am very much thankful to paper contributors of this book. It is impossible for me to edit this book without the help and co-operation of all paper writers of this book, so I am very much thankful to them.

I am also thankful to Dr. E.Raja Rao, Professor in English, Dept. of MBA, SMIT, Ankushpur, Berhampur (Orissa) for his help in editing the book.

My wife Smt. Swarnaprava Misra who has co-operated with me for all the time for editing this book and, hence, needs special mention in this list. Further I am also thankful to my two sons Roopesh and Rookesh for their encouragement to edit this book.

My special thanks are to Mr. Tilak Wasan, the Proprietor, Discovery Publishing House who readily agreed to publish the book inspite of heavy demand for publications from other quarters. I, on behalf of the paper contributors, I am very much thankful to Mr. Tilak Wasan for publishing this book. I am also very much thankful to all the staffs of the Discovery Publishing House, New Delhi for their kind help and co-operation in publishing this book in time.

Dr. Rabi Narayana Misra

Contents

Preface

Acknowledgement

1. Management Control in Road Transport Undertakings: A Study on North Bengal State Transport Corporation
Dr. Debabrata Mitra 1-7

2. Role of Surface Transport for Rural Development
P.K. Chhotroy 8-17

3. Development of Roads in Gajapati District: A Historical Perspective 18-31
Dr. Bharata Panda

4. Surface Transports in Orissa: A Look
Dr. R.N. Misra, Rookesh Kumar Misra 32-36

5. Role of Surface Transport in Rural Development: A Case Study of Phulbani District
Dr. Pradeep Pattanayak 37-47

6. Management of Surface Transport in India: A Look
Dr. Anil Kumar Sahu, Dr. R.N. Misra 48-53

7. Transport and Economic Development in Orissa
Pradip K. Brahma, R.P. Sharma 54-64

8. Rural Road: A Key Indicator for Rural Development—Study
Dr. Santosh Kumar Pradhan, Dr. Rabi Narayana Misra 65-71

9. Surface Transport for Rural Development: With Special Reference to Rural Roads
Dr. Jagabandhu Samal 72-80

10. Role of Transport in Public Sector Undertaking of Orissa: A Study of O.R.T. Co. Ltd.
Sudhansu Sekhar Nayak, Dr. Rabi Narayana Misra 81-91

11. Railway Transportation in Orissa: A Study
Prafulla Chandra Mohanty 92-104

12. Road Transport System in Orissa: A Management Look
Dr. Sudhansu Sekhar Nayak
Dr. Anil Kumar Sahu
Dr. Rabi Narayana Misra 105-112

Index *113*

1

Management Control in Road Transport Undertakings

A Study on North Bengal State Transport Corporation

Dr. Debabrata Mitra*

Abstract

With the prevailing competition, the performance of State Transport Undertakings (STUs) is deteriorating fast. State Transport Undertakings are today competing with private bus operators as well as various other modes of transport such as tempos, taxis rickshaws etc. North Bengal State Transport Corporation is not an exception to this fate. The financial position of North Bengal State Transport Corporation is deteriorating at a very fast pace. This paper is aimed at to make an elaborate discussion on different management control measures to be adopted by North Bengal State Transport Corporation for maximum utilisation of its available resources, which will go in a long way towards reducing the cost of operation.

Introduction

North Bengal State Transport Corporation was established for the purposes of providing transportation services mainly to the people of North Bengal. NBSTC has its headquarter in Coochbehar.

---

* **Reader in Commerce, University of North Bengal.**

Its branches located in various parts of North Bengal and South Bengal. Every day around two hundred buses fly from one part to another. This corporation is employing more than thousand of employees.

Presently, this corporation has been facing acute fund crisis which result in non payment of retiral benefits to its employees and even non-payment of regular salaries to its employees.

In order to overcome this problem exercise of rigid control mechanism is absolutely necessary.

Control is a management function of taking action to ensure that the plans are implemented and the targets achieved. It is an exercise to induce force to organise and implement plans and to take corrective action on the methods adopted. By measuring the results achieved the re-planning process starts, then again organise, take action and measure results—likewise the cycle continues. Therefore, it is a continuous process. This process can be explained with the help of following figure:

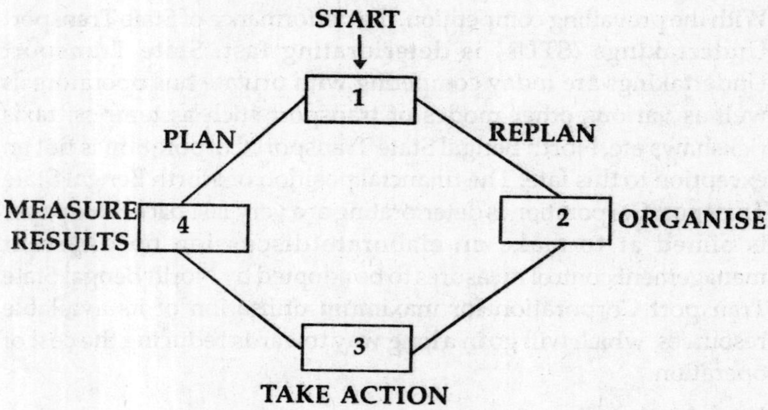

The above kind of cycle may be applied to any type of business.

What aspects it seeks to control is the efficiency of operations. To improve efficiency, we must first establish that there is inefficiency. Having done this we must analyze its causes and pin point the lack of responsibility. We then achieve efficiency by motivating the individuals responsible to remove the causes. This sounds simple, but we cannot start the process until we establish that inefficiency exists and do this we need reliable criteria or target.

We need to know, for example:

— How long each operation should take

— How much material should be used

— How much expenses should be incurred and so on our targets, therefore, take the form of Standards or Norms or budgets or Material specification or Forecast etc.

Then we will have to compare the actual time taken-actual material used, actual expenses incurred, actual volume reached etc., with the norms or targets in such a way that the cause and responsibility for any excess (in efficiency) is revealed. If comparison shows savings rather than excesses then subject to investigation, there is a possibility that the targets or norms have been too loose or have become too low because of changed circumstances or technical improvement. The targets will then have to be adjusted so that they are maintained as a fair measure of efficiency in the current circumstances.

1. Control of Management Related to Utilisation of Resources

(a) *The Government "in Business"*

The nationalization of North Bengal state Transport Corporation reflects the socialist philosophy of the Government. Although the fund of the Government is invested in this nationalized transport, its management is not the "business of the government". This does not indicate that the undertakings need not follow the business principles. It is utmost essential to follow the business principles to survive on its own besides aiming the above objectives.

(b) *Optimal utilisation of its main assets*

Optimizing the utilisation of its resources is the basic requirement for the management of public sector undertakings and more so the transport undertakings in which a formidable capital is invested. Generally about 80 per cent of the capital of North Bengal State Transport Corporation is invested in its vehicles. Optimizing the use of vehicles is generally the basic responsibility of management.

Therefore, it is absolutely essential on the part of NBSTC to improve the fleet utilisation by reducing of off-road vehicles but also increasing the vehicle utilisation by ensuring fully that all the vehicles on roads perform maximum kms.

(c) *Optimal utilisation of Crew (Drivers and Conductors)*

Optimum utilisation of the crew is measured in terms of average productivity of crew, which is generally expressed in terms of average duty hours and minutes performed by each crew on duty per day. For reducing the cost, it is absolutely essential to improve crew utilisation by extracting more duty hours from each crew. As the Motor Transport Workers Act, Motor Vehicles Act and rules restrict extracting more duty hours from crew, optimising crew utilisation in a road transport undertaking should be in terms of kilometres covered per day, besides in terms of duty hours per day.

2. Control of Management on Cost of Operations

(a) *Minimising operating costs*

In addition to make maximum use of resources in terms of vehicle and utilisation of crew, the NBSTC should also be concerned with reducing the cost of operation.

(b) *Route Economics*

As far as possible, stress must be given on selecting such routes which offer a higher and regular traffic potential together with adequate utilisation of vehicle, although it may not be possible on account of the state government policy to operate such routes for the social and economic upliftment of the rural population. The losses incurred by such operation should be known for the purpose of determining the efficiency of the undertakings as a business industry.

3. Control of Management for Minimising Operating Cost

In order to secure efficient operating costs NBSTC must establish at first where the inefficiency exist by comparing actual costs with the budgeted targets. At the time of preparation of budgets, the norms or targets for all the parameters should be worked out on the basis of experience and previous average costs. The total operating cost may be divided as under:

(a) *Staff cost:* Staff cost is about 42 per cent of the total cost. It is highly important to have a better control over the staff cost. For reducing the staff cost the following measures may be initiated:

(i) Vehicles and staff ratio should be reduced;

(ii) Maximum hours of work should be extracted;

(iii) Efforts to be made to reduce the idle labour as much as possible;

(iv) Computerisation should be done to the maximum possible level.

(b) *Fuel cost:* Fuel cost is the second largest cost in bus operation next to the staff cost. Fuel cost generally depends on the consumption of fuel. Fuel consumption is generally measured in KMPL and depends largely on driving habits of the drivers and maintenance of the vehicles. Divers must be well trained in their driving habits for the purposes of improving the fuel performance.

(c) *Tyre cost*: The third largest cost in bus operation is on tyres, tubes and flaps. The performance of tyres depends on to a large extent on the maintenance systems/ practice. With the reduction of one paise per km. In the cost of operations there will be savings of near about Rs. One Crore per annum.

(d) *Cost on spares and Assemblies:* Cost on spares and assemblies depends to a large extent on consumption and consumption depends on the maintenance practices followed by the organisation. It is measured in terms of cost per km. By following regular maintenance practices, the consumption of spares and assemblies will certainly come down and the average cost will also be reduced. The reduction of just one paise will result in an overall savings of about 1 crore in the cost on spares and assemblies.

4. Improved Quality of Public Transport Services

After the amendment of Motor Vehicles Act, 1988 and the liberal policy adopted by both the Central and State Governments, a number of private operators have started their operation into the transport field. As the private operators are trying to attract passengers by providing new and comfortable vehicles, the operations of NBSTC are badly affected and its earnings have dropped considerably.

In the present day, passengers want door-to-door service with all the travelling comforts. With the availability of multiple modes of transport, passengers can choice of their own. Thus, the market has become the buyers market. Now the situation has become so much competitive that the NBSTC for its survival has to compete with the private operators only by improving the quality of its services.

Conclusion

Management of NBSTC must have to adopt controlling measures to improve the efficiency and performance of this undertaking. They should put stress on the optimum utilisation of the assets in order to improve the productivity of both vehicles and crew. As it would not be possible to augment duty hours of the crew on account of the limitation imposed by the Motor Vehicles Act and Motor Transport Workers Act, efforts must be made to increase the utilisation in terms of kms. operated. Effort should be made to reduce the cost per km. to the maximum possible extent. State Government should make its best possible effort in order to bring the concept of "cost consciousness" in the mind of employees and managers of NBSTC.

This is the time when NBSTC is required to increase its occupancy by laying emphasis both on comfortable travel and amenities at bus stations. A strict control on both men and material often by motivation and at times by resorting to penal action in case of failures is utmost necessary to make this industry "an industry surviving to last".

REFERENCES

1. BT: Business Today, 1998, *Competitiveness and Micro-economics*, September 22: pp. 96-101.

2. Chandra P., Sustry, T., 1998, *Competitiveness of Indian Manufacturing Vikalppa*, Vol. 23, No.3. July-September, pp. 25-36.

3. Daveshwar, Y.C., 1999 Strides Towards Competitiveness, *Business Today*, August 22.

4. Eccles, R.G., 1991, The Performance Measurement Manifesto, *Harvard Business Review*, Jan-Feb pp. 131-137.

5. Kotler Philip 1974, What Consumer Mean for Markets? *Harvard Business Review*, May-June, p. 4a.

6. Nadaf A.M. 2002, Management Control in Road Transport Undertaking, *Indian Journal of Transport Management*, April-June, pp. 234-246.

7. Porter M.E. 1996. What is Strategy? *Harvard Business Review*, 74(b), pp. 61-78.

8. Prahalad, C.K. and Hamel, G, 1990, the Core Competence of the Corporation, *Harvard Business Review*, May-June pp. 79-91.

9. Tracey, M., Vonderembse, M.A and Lim, Jeen-Su, 1999, Manufacturing Technology and Strategy Formulation. Keys to Enhance Competitiveness and Improving Performance, *Journal of Operations Management*, pp. 411-428.

10. *Various Published Reports* of North Bengal State Transport Corporation.

11. Williams, J.R., 1992, How Sustainable is your Competitive Advantage? *California Management Review, Spring* pp. 29-51.

2

Role of Surface Transport for Rural Development

P.K. Chhotroy*

Some of the developmental issues that cannot be fully accomplished without proper development of surface transport along with other infrastructure support are as follows:

(i) Diversifying production and expanding trade;

(ii) Coping with population and reducing poverty/enhancing employment;

(iii) Raising productivity and lowering cost;

(iv) Efficient resource allocation;

(v) Improving environmental condition.

Roads Lead to Economic Prosperity

Extensive studies undertaken by international bodies like the World Bank, established that 1 per cent increase in investment in the stock of infrastructure, leads to a corresponding 1 per cent increase of the gross domestic product of a nation.[1] Von oppen (1982, 83a, 1983b) showed that market infrastructure has a measurable and significant positive effect on increasing the agricultural productivity. He tried to demonstrate how the geographical accessibility to markets can increase the productivity and it is said to be as high as 5 times and suggests the expansion of

* **Sri P.K. Chhotroy, M.A., Retd. Principal, Gunupur College, Gunupur.**

the system.[2] Indeed, there is a direct correlation between the creation of connectivity infrastructure, notably roads and development. This correlation holds good in terms of poverty alleviation as well. States with poor connectivity are also the states that reflect poor socio-economic indices. It is well appreciated by now that the green revolution occurred earlier in the areas having a network of roads linking the input supply depots and output marketing yards like mandis with villages. In Punjab, the state which recorded the fastest agricultural growth from 1970 onwards, the road network increased from around 13900 kms in 1970 to 40,000 kms by 1995s. The length of rural roads increased from about 16000 kms to over 30,000 kms during the same period. By the mid-1995 the state had acquired 100 per cent rural road connectivity. The number of trucks operating in Punjab rose from a mere 2000 in 1970 to around 20,000 by 1980 and further up to over 58,000 by the mid-1990. The number of tractors went up from 56,600 in the mid-1970s to over 3,87,000 by the mid-1990s. Another example of how the laying down of roads helps in ushering in economic prosperity through farm and off-farm income generation activities is provided by a study of villages in Meerut district of Uttar Pradesh. The study (conducted by Rita Sharma and Thomas T. Poleman and published in a book form by the Vikas Publishers) clearly brought out that spread of vegetable and potato cultivation in villages was facilitated chiefly by the network of roads and transport that allowed the produce to be marketed in time. In one village Izarpur, four private milk traders and co-operative milk collection centres began operating after its linkage with road. The mobility of the village population improved appreciably with the development of road and transport infrastructure. Labour contractors started coming the village with trucks to transport workers to the construction sites. Self employment through investment in cycle-rickshaws and tempo-taxies for hire became possible. A network of service establishments came up to maintain the growing transport sector.[3]

Status of Transport Infrastructure

The road transport services as well as railways occupy a prominent place in our economy accounting for 52.3 per cent and 13.7. per cent respectively of the total sector.[4] Road Transport is the dominant mode of transport in the country. There is a consumers preference for this mode of transport as it has inherent advantages of timeliness in the movement of goods and passengers and provides door to door service if needed. The freight traffic moved by roads have grown rapidly compared to those by rail. The share of roads has increased to 60 per cent in freight in 1995 from 11 per cent in 1952, similarly in passenger traffic it has increased to 80 per cent form 28 per cent in 1952.[5] Recent studies undertaken by the planning commission and the national productivity council on the status of the development of transport infrastructure in major states highlights the prevalence of greater disparity amongst different states. Table 2.1 Provides the details:

Table 2.1: Status of transport infrastructure development in India

Feature	*All India*	*Spread amongst States*	*States at Extreme*
Railway route length (Kilometre per 1000 sq.km) (1993-94)	19.0	47.7-12.9	Maharastra, Orissa
Road Length (Kilometre per 1000 Sq.Km. (1988-89)	584	5472-289	Kerala, Madhya Pradesh
Motor Vehicle per 1000 population	285	733-127	Punjab, Bihar

Yojana, Jan., 1998. p. 15.

It is found that, state with higher per capita income appear to make better progress in transport infrastructure development and thus higher per capita income in the state.

Rural Connectivity

Only a few states like Kerala, Punjab and Goa can talk of 100 per cent rural connectivity, whereas many other states are far behind the target (See Appendix). An expert group was set up in the Ministry of Rural Development which reviewed the existing national norms for rural roads and recommended 100 per cent linkage to villages with population over 500 and 50 per cent linkage to villages with population between 200 to 500 in hilly areas. As far as tribal, coastal and desert are concerned, the committee recommended 100 per cent linkage to villages with population over 1000 and 75 per cent linkage to villages with population below 1000. A time frame of ten years was proposed to achieve the above target.

The task of developing rural roads is entrusted to state governments. But the information available in this regard is not complete. Many states do not have data regarding physical and financial progress of rural roads under minimum needs programme. Data on the length of the roads constructed, number of villages connected and expenditure incurred is also incomplete because of lack of co-ordination between different agencies involved in the task. "Rural roads tell a story of neglect. The information relating to their development is incomplete and there is also lack of co-ordination between different agencies involved in the task. In addition to the need for providing substantial funds for their development, it is necessary to evolve a proper monitoring mechanism to have updated data to enable better planning and development. [6]

Gap in Rural Transportation Demand and Accessibility

Transportation in rural areas is a giant task in India as the 5,98,317 villages are scattered widely over a vast area of 33 lakh sq. km. The demand for rural goods transport infrastructure has to handle 10 lakh tonnes of inward traffic and 4000 lakh tonnes of outward traffic, in addition to the passenger transport requirements. But much of the rural road length of over 18.2 lakh km is in a dilapidated condition, as it is not able to meet the existing and expected traffic demand.[7]

Vision for Rural Development

The government of India's vision for rural road development during the 20 year period from 2001 to 2021is incorporated in the vision document.[8] According to statistics, while only 28 per cent of the total 5.89 lakh villages were connected with roads till 1980, a massive investment of Rs. 15,000 crores for development of rural roads during the succeeding 20 years helped in raising this percentage to 54. The value of the rural road asset as of now is estimated to be over Rs. 100,000 crore. This is remarkable achievement for a nation of our size. However, the challenges for future development are formidable, as even 53 years of independence are over, 46 per cent of our villages are yet to be provided with all weather roads. The vision document proposes development and implementation of master plans at district levels and gives targets of achieving accessibility to villages with population above 1000 by 2003, between 500 and 1000 by 2007 and below 500 by 2010.

Innovative Technology for Rural Roads

Considering the equipment and material constraints, concrete block pavement/inter locking concrete block pavement has been developed for the pavement construction in rural areas. This is a newly emerging technology with simplified construction method. The technology requires only low investment, enables use of local materials, provides avenues for rural employment in block production and laying, uses locally available skills in brick laying and helps to enhance such skills. It is an appropriate technology for rural road development. It can play a crucial role in achieving the objective of sustainable development of rural roads.[9]

Pradhan Mantri Gram Sadak Yojana (PMGSY)

In tune with the objectives of the Road Development plan vision, a national mission for achieving rural connectivity through provision of all-weather roads to remote villages was initiated by PMGSY in 2001, with the objectives of connecting all villages having population more than 500 by the year 2007. This is an ambitious programme for the nation's economy in general and the rural economy in particular. It is expected that, through the implementation of this programme, out of the 3,50,000 unconnected habitations, 1,60,000 habitations will be benefited, with the construction of some 6,00,000 km. of new all-weather roads. Thus, the successful execution of this programme will lead to a quantum jump in the nations economy.[10] Since the local self governments in the form of Zilla Parishads will be actively involved in the planning and implementation of the programme, there is scope for peoples participation at the grassroot level.

Conclusion

Development of rural roads is the catalyst for allround development of the rural community. However, it is a stupendous task for a country of our size to provide universal access through roads and reap the benefits of rural economy can be enhanced when due attention is given to the errors of past and the needs of the present. Considering the multifarious effect of rural connectivity on the over-all socio-economic development of the villages the key suggestions are:

(i) Growth of self-sufficient village economy, unlike the colonial extraction of resources from villages;

(ii) provision of a network of supporting activities as mere roads are not enough. The productivity of road system depends on tonnes of freight carried per km. and number of vehicles on road per kilometre. Liberal finance should be made available to the cultivators of tribal area and the marine fishermen of coastal Orissa to have their own processing, storage and transport facilities. The youth organizations of tribal area and the SAMUDRAM of costal Orissa can be engaged in this field. Efforts should be made to establish direct link with the consumers, so that the manipulative power of the whole sale dealers can be brought under control;

(iii) The future agenda should ensure sustainable development of both rural economy and rural roads and intellectually challenging to attract and retain youth in this important avocation.

APPENDIX—2.1

Village Connectivity with Population Less than 1000

Sl. No.	*States/ UTs*	*No. of Villages*	*Villages connected upto 1991-92*	*Balance to be connected*
1.	Andhra Pradesh	13888	4504	9384
2.	Arunachal Pradesh	3176	612	2564
3.	Assam	18777	11362	7415
4.	Bihar	53234	14457	38777
5.	Goa	172	172	0
6.	Gujarat	9814	7362	2452
7.	Haryana	3275	3209	66
8.	Himachal Pradesh	NA		
9.	Jammu & Kashmir	NA		
10.	Karnataka	18632	6399	12233
11.	Kerala		All connected...	
12.	Madhya Pradesh	63546	13982	49564
13.	Maharastra	25057	6381	18676
14.	Manipur	1760	695	1065
15.	Meghalaya	4793	80	4613
16.	Mizoram	395	287	108
17.	Nagaland	NA		
18.	Orissa	41132	11428	29704
19.	Punjab	8842	8729	133
20.	Rajasthan	27598	6655	20943
21.	Sikkim	371	234	137
22.	Tamil Nadu	19867	11996	7871
23.	Tripura	4183	3120	1063
24.	Uttar Pradesh	90271	31762	58509
25.	West Bengal	27646	11004	16642
26.	A&N Islands	460	223	237
27.	Chandigarh	0	0	0
28.	D&N Haveli	34	30	4
29.	Daman &Diu	11	11	0
30.	Delhi	54	54	0
31.	Lakshadweep	0	0	0
32.	Pondicherry	207	207	0
	All India	**437195**	**154955**	**282160**

Source: Compedium of Transport Statistics, Planning Commission, January, 1993.

APPENDIX—2.2

Village Connectivity with Population 1000-1500

Sl. No.	*States/UTs*	*No.of villages*	*Villages connected upto 1991-92*	*Balance to be connected*
1.	Andhra Pradesh	3767	2192	1575
2.	Arunachal Pradesh	49	36	13
3.	Assam	1907	1907	0
4.	Bihar	6104	3104	3000
5.	Goa	100	100	0
6.	Gujarat	3249	3073	176
7.	Haryana	1160	1159	1
8.	Himachal Pradesh	263	218	45
9.	Jammu & Kashmir	611	499	112
10.	Karnataka	3461	2384	1077
11.	Kerala	10	10	0
12.	Madhya Pradesh	4427	2852	1575
13.	Maharashtra	5143	4623	520
14.	Manipur	110	95	15
15.	Meghalaya	64	64	0
16.	Mizoram	286	286	0
17.	Nagaland	132	116	46
18.	Orissa	3524	2817	707
19.	Punjab	1657	1657	0
20.	Rajasthan	2407	1690	717
21.	Sikkim	48	40	8
22.	Tamil Nadu	2514	2216	298
23.	Tripura	235	170	65
24.	Uttar Pradesh	11396	7059	4337
25.	West Bengal	5500	3494	2006
26.	A &N Islands	16	16	0
27.	Chandigarh	3	3	0
28.	D &N Haveli	13	13	0
29.	Daman & Diu	5	5	0
30.	Delhi	37	37	0
31.	Lakshadweep	0	0	0
32.	Pondicherry	31	31	0
	All India	**58229**	**41966**	**16263**

Source: Compendium of Transport Statistics, Planning Commission, January, 1993.

APPENDIX—2.3

Village Connectivity with Population 1000-1500

Sl. No.	*States/UTs*	*No.of villages*	*Villages connected upto 1991-92*	*Balance to be connected*
1.	Andhra Pradesh	9700	9231	469
2.	Arunachal Pradesh	32	31	1
3.	Assam	1812	1812	0
4.	Bihar	8228	5333	2895
5.	Goa	126	101	25
6.	Gujarat	5051	5010	41
7.	Haryana	2310	2309	1
8.	Himachal Pradesh	196	178	18
9.	Jammu & Kashmir	567	520	47
10.	Karnataka	4935	4111	824
11.	Kerala	1252	1252	0
12.	Madhya Pradesh	2910	2670	240
13.	Maharashtra	6185	6100	85
14.	Manipur	167	165	2
15.	Meghalaya	45	45	0
16.	Mizoram	56	56	0
17.	Nagaland	108	108	0
18.	Orissa	2649	2629	20
19.	Punjab	1689	1689	0
20.	Rajasthan	3300	3091	209
21.	Sikkim	21	21	0
22.	Tamil Nadu	3918	3877	41
23.	Tripura	300	300	0
24.	Uttar Pradesh	10899	10447	452
25.	West Bengal	4928	3008	1920
26.	A&N Islands	15	15	0
27.	Chandigarh	13	13	0
28.	D&N Haveli	25	25	0
29.	Daman & Diu	10	10	0
30.	Delhi	123	123	0
31.	Lakshadweep	0	0	0
32.	Pondicherry	53	53	0
	All India	**71623**	**64333**	**7290**

Source: Compendium of Transport Statistics, Planning Commission, January,1993.

REFERENCES

1. Khader, S.A. Quoted in the Article, "Productivity in Infrastructure" *Yojana*, January 1998, p. 13.
2. Von Oppen Quoted in the Article "Agricultural Marketing Status, Future Policies and Strategies" by Prof. D. Shrijaya Vebaraj Vrs. *Kurukshetra*, October 2002. p. 50.
3. Seed, Surinder, Rural Connectively Current Issues and Future Plans. *Kurukshetra*, October 2002, p. 70.
4. Narain Yogendra, New Initiatives in Infrastructure Sector, *Yojana*, January 1998, p. 5.
5. Prasad Mahesh Roads: The Task Ahead, *Yojana*, January 1998, p. 63.
6. Bhagyalakshmi, J. Rural Roads: Vital Link to Prosperity, *Yojana*, January 1998. p. 67.
7. Rao, D.P. &Rao, B.R. Agricultural Commodity Transportation in India, Inter-India Publications 1947, p. 88.
8. Ministry of Road Transport and Highways: Road Development Plan Vision 2001 Ministry of Transport and Highways. Published by *Indian Road Congress*. (2001), 41.
9. Muraleedharam, T& Sood V.K.: Innovative Technology for Rural Roads, *Kurukshetra* November 2003, p. 48.
10. Sikdar P.K.: Pradhan Mantri Gram Sadak Yojana—A Mission for Rural Connectivity by All Weather Roads, *Indian Highways*. Vol. 29, No. 5 (May, 2001), 81, Pradhan Mantri Gram Sadak Yojana-For the People, *Indian Highways*, Vol. 30, No. 6. (June 2002), 59.

3

Development of Roads in Gajapati District

A Historical Perspective

Dr. Bharata Panda*

The roads of rural area can be classified into two: (1) Roads in plain area and (2) Roads in Hill tracts. The infrastructure required for rural development is the communication, irrigation and education. The socio-economic condition which includes culture can reach its target if the above infrastructure is developed. How the communication helped to witness the outer world can be examined taking a single area like Gajapati District.

The Eastern Ghats constitute one of the principal mountain systems of Orissa state. The hills and their associated features roughly extend over 1.15 lakh sq kms. of the area i.e. 75 per cent of the total area of the state. It is the home of nearly 15 million people (nearly 50 per cent of the total population of the state) out of which 75 per cent are tribals. The ghat's forest resources have been a perennial source of their subsistence.

The physiographic section of Gajapati district between the rivers of Rusikulya and Nagawali lie Maliyas, Mahendragiri Hills, Vansadhara and Niyamgiri Hills. The important mountains and peaks with their altitude are Singarazu Parvat 1516 feet, Niyamgiri

* **Bharata Panda, Ph.D, former Principal, Parsuram Gurukul Mahavidyalaya, Sevakpur, Mayuree Nagar, H.No.51, Nilachala Nagar 3rd Lane, Brahmapur, 760010, Ganjam.**

1515 feet, Mahendragiri 1501 feet, Devgiri 1382 feet, Chandragiri 1269 feet, Subarnagiri 1257 feet, Kotangi since 1172 feet, Kirimbatheali 1100 feet, Giridabadi 1036 feet, Raigara Hill 881 feet and Deomali 1672 feet. All are situated south of Tel river and west of river Nagawali. (Patro and Panda, 1994).

According to the Survey of India map S.N. Rajguru refers to one Nasunda parvat in line 18 of the Tekkali inscription of Madhyamaraja. Sarat Chandra Behera says that Rajguru however identifies this hill with Nandava forest. He writes Nasunda Parvata of the verse may be taken to be the hill near Nandava forest is in the modern Gajapati district, very near to the boundary between Parlakhemundi and Tekkali. This Nandava forest is about three or four miles away from Tekkalipatna. The Nandava Hills are so full of natural beauties and are connected with Mahendra Parvata by a range of hills called Durga and Labanyagado that they are called the crest jewel of Odra Desha.

The Maliahs or high lands of Ganjam composed of a series of undulating plateau, contain the highest peaks, named Singaraju and Mahendragiri which rise to a height of nearly 5000 feet above the sea. Many passes lead into these hills, and include the Kalinga Ghat from Rrussellkonda, The Munising Ghat from Parlakhemundi and the Taptapani or hot spring Ghat so named from its containing a hot sulphir spring. The Maliahs are inhabited among others by Kondhas, Savaras Gonds and Pano Hill weaves. (Thruston, 1913) The entire Gajapati District from Mohana to Kasinagar Block comes under sub tropical climate. Mahendragiri is located at the centre of the district.

The flora of Mahendragiri quiet interesting because its subtropical climate has favoured the development of some species of the lower Himalayas. The South Indian mountains make their presence in Mahendragiri, thereby indicating that these hills form an intermediate step for the migration of species from lower Himalayas to south Indian Mountain and or/vice versa (M.Brahman and Saxena, 1993).

During the feudal regime and the British rule the whole of Ganjam Maliahs was a State of insurrection and rebellion, disorder and violence. Ganjam Agency area comprises the Development Blocks of Mohana, Gumma, Rayagada, Nuagada, R. Udayagiri and the Sorada Taluk excluding Pandakhol mutha. Ganjam Agency as identified above consisting five out of seven Development Blocks of old Parlakhemundi Sub-division now called Gajapati district. (ITDA, 2002). Up to 1766, Ad this agency area was neglected and isolated from the rest of India due to disturbance and violence. No roads and communication was there except cart routes and walking hill tracts to attend the weekly market and pilgrimage.

The English received the whole of Northern Circars in 1766, in which the Gajapati district was included. Mr. Cots Ford an engineer of the East India Company came to Ganjam as resident to conduct a survey in 1767 and faced the disturbance condition in Parlakhemundi Zamindary, which was the largest and most important monarchy in Ganjam district. The of Parlakhemundi Jagannath Gajapati Narayan Dev along with other dissatisfied Zamidars and tannest created hindrance and intercepted all communication between Bengal to Madras. To stop the political disturbance the English applied force and constructed the roads between 1767 and 1803. They tried their best to construct the roads for commercial purpose and to take military action in the rural areas. The area was administered under Madras Presidency. During British rule in India the roads were constructed mostly for the purpose to suppress the revolution and to collect land revenue.

The Parlakimidi Rebellion started in 1813 and continued up to 1832. In December 1832 George Russell was appointed as Special Commissioner to deal with the situation. He applied Marshal Law and some Bishoyis were hanged, many of the rebels were captured, 25 of them were hanged, 25 were sentenced to transportation for life and 103 were sent to Velor Jail as state prisoners. The resistance movements in Parlakhemundi ended in this way, which was started in 1768 ended in 1884.

During the period of British rule there were 503 villages in Parlakhemundi estate providing land revenue to the tune of Rs. 2, 78,720. The estate was divided into 24 Muthas and 11 Bishoyis or feudal chieftains of which 7 have their forts in the Maliahs and 4 in the plains at Gumma, Rayagada, Jiranga, Seranga, Ajayagodo, Komalsingh, Koinpur, Namanagaram, Gandahati, Narayanapuram and Lahuniagodo.

The above mentioned 11 Muthas or the hill chief was given special Sanandas for permanent settlement of their estates. The services required of them was originally of military character, but in course of time their duties became confined to maintain of Law and Order giving timely information of disturbances and offences and maintenances of roads and Bungalows etc. They had inam lands. They had the right to collect dues from the tribal villages under their jurisdiction, and known as Muthas or Fort. Bishoyis are the chief. They used to collect the following from the tribal people. (Pattnaik, 1983).

1. Paik's and peshnia's mamul
2. Village servants' mamul
3. Supply of Dhalia to Khemundi Royal family
4. Unfair Labour of labour without payment of wages. (Called Bethipaiti)

The Maliahas were subdivided into Muthas and each Mutha was incharge of a Mutha head variously called patro Bissoyi or Naik, etc., according to custom prevailing in each Maliaha. They number and name of Muthas contained in each Maliaha is Given below:

List of Muthas

Sl. No.	*Name of taluk*	*Name of Muthas*	*No. of villages*
1	*2*	*3*	*4*
1.	R.Udayagiri....	Udayagiri-88, Ramagiri-54, Badapada-7, Khajuripada-8 Jhalarsinga-4, Nuagodo-20 Parimala-5, Udayapur N.A-6 Cheligada-17, Mahendragada-5 Titisingi-14, Keradango-10 Ranalai N.A.-2, Cheligada-10 Ambogaon N.A-20, Deraba-5 Padmapur-1, Tumba N.A-9 Karudal-,Dhepiguda N.A-6, Sialilati N.A-23, Godru-3, and Total:-317	

(Contd...)

1	*2*	*3*	*4*
2.	Mohana...	Gobindapur-27, Karachabadi-12, Kondhodaba-21, Mohana-50 Buduli-11, Adova-42, Birikota-33 Pandiguda N.A.-43, Jhilliko-15 Chandragiri-117, Chandiput-8 Jarrow-40, Goudagotho N.A.-16, Marikote N.A.-29, Kulaba N.A.-43 Luhagudi-48...Total:-555	
3.	Parlakhemundi...	Labanyakota-25, Gandahati-21, Saba & Doborasingi-34 Rayagada-64, Jiranga-40, Narayanapur-18 Koinpur-15, Serango-32, Gumma-96, Ajagodo-33... Total: 390	
4.	Soroda...	Pandakhol-28 Total:- 28	
5.	Bramhapur	Tunba-21 Totals:- 21	
		Grand Total:- 1411	

The Roads in the Parlakhemundi estates were constructed during English period as follows:

Road	*No. in miles*
1	*2*
Gumma Road from Baranasi Road to Munisingi village	9
Palam and Temburu Road	9
Road from Chapara on the Punch Road To Kinchilingi via Garabandha	12
Nowtala Road	7
Gyba Road	7
Tekkalipatnam and Goppili Road	6
Kimidi and Patapuram Road	13
Kimidi and Kinchiling Road	20
Garabandha and Goppili Road	6
Singapuram and Goppili Road	9

(Contd...)

1	2
Gosani Road	5.5
Road from Zamindar's palace to Burugam	3.75
Road Kanchuru to Basaba via Valunda	7
Road Gusadi to Buskudi	2.25
Road from Uppalada and Kimidi and Kinchilingi Road to Gajapati Sagaram tank	3.25

Besides the above roads the following roads were the main communication network: Parlakhemundi to Kalingapatnam, Noupada- Hiramandalam-Temburu, Pundi-Mukhalingam-Chintada-Gara etc. (Maltby, 1918) (All these roads now are in Andhra Pradesh). Roads to Uddan or (Udayan Khandam) Aruna Charan Ghat, Road from Rayagada to Udayagiri, Ghat Road from Rayagada to Mahendragiri through Angar Ghati, Bangoroba, Jirango, Koinpur-Gandahati,- Goppili were also constructed during British rule.

The permanent settlement of the estate was made in 1801; at the same time the management of other states as Court of Wards commenced in 1830. Parlakhemundi Maliah track was returned to its Zmindar which had a population of 19,201 chiefly Savaras, covering an area of 350 square miles. Eighteen hill schools were established, fourteen under the special Agents and two each under the Principal and Senior Assistant Agents. The schools were attended by 735 boys and 11 girls; of the boys 117 were Khonds, 3 Savaras and rest were Uriyas. (Ganjam Manual, 1878)

A tribal looks upon the farms as its natural environment. He needs forest for his food, shelter, clothing and medicines, the basic needs. During community festivals, spiritual rights and rituals are very much interlinked with the forest. The jungles even though it was under the control of Zamindar, the new Madras Forest Act of 1882 created disturbances afresh in the area. Hence forest roads were constructed. Up to the end of revolution the Savaras were in a disturbed condition.

The Savaras who live undisturbed in the hill tracts their retreat was gradually exposed them to the outside influence. Many outsiders infiltrated into the tribal areas as soon as they were opened up with the development of road communication and establishment of market centres. They started exploiting the Savaras by acquiring their land and extracting from them manual labour by various illegal means. Being oppressed, exploited and deprived of their land, property and freedom, the Savras, many a time rose in revolt against the outside agencies. The local hill chiefs for some reasons or other, started fighting with one another. When the situation in the tribal areas turned from bad to worse, the British authorities, who took possession of these areas, stamped out the tribal rebellion with an iron hand and maintained law and order throughout their sojourn in India. They were not only concerned with the maintenance of law and order for peace and good government in tribal areas, but were also interested in developing the tribals and protecting them from all forms of exploitation. Some of the measures of improvement were construction of road, establishment of schools, hospitals, market centres and administrative headquarters. These ameliorative measures did more harm than good to the tribals because they encouraged more infiltration by moneylenders and merchants than before. As a result the discontentment and frustration among the people were intensified without any means of resolving them from each of any strong internal leadership. (Pattnaik, 1983).

The tribals of Ganjam have started seeing the light and now in most of the pockets demonstrate a sense of zeal and vigour under the impact of special tribal development projects. One integrated Tribal Development agency is in operation in Parlakhemundi. Besides this there are three micro projects. Lanjia. Saora Development Agency at Tumba has been established for the development of the primitive section of the Saora tribe. Some of the schemes which promise great prospects of development, in fact have already made a dent in bringing about change for the betterment in the economic condition of the tribal people are: (1) hill slope development (2) plantation in Serango area (3) water harvesting and land development in Chandragiri and Tumba areas. The hidden infrastructure which is required to carry forward the programmes of tribal development is the administrative structure comprising a band of dedicated workers and whatever progress had so far been achieved in tribal development are products of their hard labour *Bohidar*, 1983.

After Independence the Government in 1949 abolished all the mamools except sanja sistu mamool, subsequently in 1964 Government fixed the said mamool instead of in kind at a flat rate of Rupee one peer acre. Mutha head system has been abolished in 1969 in the agency tracts. Only the cultivating classes are continuing after the abolition of Mutha-Head system. Survey and settlement operation have been taken up for the first time in accordance with the Revenue Department in 1964 and operation were carried out as per Orissa Survey and Settlement Act of 1958. (Panda, 1983)

Mohana, Nuagada, R. Udayagiri, Rayagada and Gumma blocks are the scheduled blocks called sub plan areas for development was declared during Eight Five year Plan. Besides this, H & T.I Department, I.T.D.A Programmes, special welfare wing, I.T.D.A. programmes, special development agencies are formed in for the Rural Development. Infrastructure development and education was given toper priority. Special projects are also in the action plan for development of agriculture and horticulture. The Soara development Agency at Chandragiri is fully alerted for socio-economic development of the Tribals of the district. *(Pani 2001)*

Reservation of vacancies for candidates belonging to S.C and S.T. in public schools issued in 1963. For the implementation of horticulture and irrigation the importance has given for the development of village link roads. A central sponsored scheme called National Watershed Development Project in rain fed areas (NWDPRA) has been started during 1990-91. One micro watershed has been selected in each Block on a pilot scale for integrated treatment through different departments like Agriculture, Horticulture, Forest, and Veterinary. Since inception of the soil conservation activities in 1971-72 a number of soil conservation measures have been taken up.(Rao, 1992)

"When Peninsular India first came under the British rule, the roads suitable for wheeled traffic an existed in this part of the country. The only "made' roads in these days were the rough roads opened originally for the passage of troops and artillery until 1813, Roads for non-Military purposes were neither constructed nor any systematic progress achieved for some years thereafter. (Ganjam District Gazetteers) Madras local board's act of 1884 superseded the act 1871.& up to 1910 District board maintained the roads. In

19th century the roads of this District divided into two categories. 1. Roads in the plains and 2. Roads, hill tracts are Maliahs. The following are the important roads of Gajapati.

Kalinga Patnam to Parlakhemundi via Narsanapeta. 15 miles (24 kms.)

Nuapada to Parlakhemundi...12 miles (19 kms.)

Pundi to Varanasi (Kasinagar) via Parlakhemundi..10 miles (16 kms.)

Taptapani ghat from Digapahandi to Luhagudi, Puipani Ghat, from Surangi via Nuagada, to Cheligada and Munisingi Ghat in Parlakhemundi, from Parlakhemundi to Gumma were all passable by loaded elephants and horses and men. The most important road which a traversed the length of Maliah from Baliguda to Gumma was known as Grand Military Road. There were mud bungalows at most of the usual halting places (Ganjam District Gazetteers)

Post Independence road communication under district board of Ganjam are: Major District roads 59.

Parlakhemundi to Gumma from the State Highway No. 4 at Parlakhemundi and proceeded upto Gumma where it is classified village road. The road preceded further to join the major district Road No. 60 at Khajuripada. All weather and block 'topped road' is about 33 kms.

Major District Road No 60: Starts from State Highway No. 4 at Parlakhmundi and proceeded via Rayagada, Khajuripada and Chandragiri at State Highway No. 17 at Luhagudi. This is an important road connects Brahmapur to Parlakhemundi (all whether black topped road 'under six kms.'

Major District Road No. 60-A: Chandiput Mohona and Adava-Paniganda (Kandhamala dist) Chandiput to Mohona 9 kms., Adova to border of Panikonda 20 kms., all whether road (5 kms. blocked topped, 15 kms. water bound, macadam surface)

The list of village roads on metalled approach road during 1985-86- Narayanpur to Jiranga road 11.600 kms. (all whether 7.300 WBM-4300BT), Ramagiri Jirango road 19 kms. (5 WBM, 14NM) Jarada Tumba road 13 kms. fair weather NM, Gosani-Gurandi-Lingipur-Uppalada road 9.60 kms. (fair weather 3.200 kms. WBM-

6.40 kms. NM) Parlakhemundi Narse peta 1 km allweather BT, Cheligada Ramagiri road 13, all weather BT, Khajuripada Nuagada Seranga road 18 kms. (fair weather 11 kms. WBM -2 kms. BT per cent km NM), Jirango Koinpur Burukhat Paas Ananda Tumban Road 35.40 kms. (fair weather 7 kms. WBM -11 kms. BT-17.40 NM) Mohana Govindpur road 29 kms. (fair weather 21 kms WBM 8 kms. NM).

Besides the above roads, Forest roads are constructed about 160 kms connected to the main villages and roads of Gajapati, during 1985-86.

The roads constructed up to dated, even though not located ample progress is seen living aside the neglected areas.

The district of Gajapati was formed on the basis of 1991 census, data of old Parlakhemundi sub-division on 1992. This Zamindar could see 150 miles pucca road along with the connection with the muthas, Tahasil, Blocks link roads constructed during British rule. Till now all sorts of repair work has been taken up in the active plan. But the interior part of Gumma-Serango, Puttara -Ramgiri, Mohana-Adava, Nuagada - R.Udayagiri, Gangabad- Madha area are neglected, for example Madha village of Singaraj can be examined. No inspection officer is able to climb up easily to this place. Hence the development work is on pen and paper could be expected. The volunteer organization is also struggling hard in the low ghats.

The Ganjam Agency-population (1971)

Name of the Block	*Area in sq.km.*	*Population*	*Sch. Tribe pop.*
Rayagada		48103	36969
Gumma		43837	31460
Nuagada	2980.11	23515	18613
R. Udayagiri		31400	20581
Mohana		63482	38608
Total			
Ganjam Agency	2980.11	2,10,337	1,46,231

Gajapati District Population 2001: (Census of India)			*M*	*F*
20 Gajapati T	CD Block	5,18,837	1,28,679	1,34,797
20 Gajapati R	CD Block	4,65,949	1,27,779	1,34,127
20 Gajapati U	CD Block	52,888	900	670
Mohana R	CD Block	115,808	32,139	33105
R. Udayagiri R	CD Block	55,010	18,628	18,660
Nuagada R	CD Block	46,936	17,453	18,512
Gumma R	CD Block	65,292	23,223	25,322
Kasi Nagar R	CD Block	48,625	7,798	8,063
Parlakhemundi (Gosani)R	CD Block	70,302	4,266	4,290
Rayagada R	CD Block	63,976	24,272	26,175
Parlakhemundi (M) TU	CD Block	43,097	862	629
Kasinagar Nac TU	CD Block	9,791	38	41

It is seen from the Census that the ST population Figure is: 2,63,476 and SC Population 38,928. Which is the dist have 51 per cent Tribal population and 8 per cent SC Population. Savara, Saura, Lanjia & Kandha comes under major tribal group of rural areas.

Tribal demography of Gajapati district is prominent and the development of those rural areas should be sustainable. In general, tribals and forests are closely associated with each other. Forests are their home of Tribal people; they used to have many traditional rights over the forests. They earn their lively food from forest. They depended on forests for almost everything. They protected the forests and forests protected them.

Over the years different tribal communities have emerged which are no longer amenable to the traditional tribal discipline. Their tribal values have eroded leading to ecological instability. They are neglected by the Forest Department, exploited by the settlers and corrupted by the plainsmen. Illegal felling, smuggling, grazing, forest fire and cutting of branches of trees for fuel are some of the examples of the activities of the tribal which have adverse impact on the eco-system.

The tribal also became victims in the hands of plainsmen who are responsible for forest destruction on a massive scale. People from the nearby villages and towns have encroached upon the tribal land in forests. They have exploited the forest resources causing ecological imbalance. Over exploitation of wild life products, killing of animals and taking out the precious medicinal plants from the forests by the plainsmen have adversely affected the life-style of tribes an it has also affected the ecological balance. It must be remembered that any activity affecting forests has its impact on the tribal life. Similarly any activity affecting the tribal people will also have an impact on the forest environment. Therefore, it is necessary that programmes of forest protection should be designed taking into consideration the tribals and ensuring their involvement. They can be involved in forest protection programmes. Their recruitment as watchmen and guards can be first step in this direction.

The National Forest Policy of 1988 has realized the need to associate tribals in forest development. In the policy statement it is stated that "having regard to the symbiotic relationship between the tribal people and forests, a primary task of all agencies responsible for forest management, including the forest development corporations should be to associates the tribal people closely in the protection. Regeneration and development of forest is taken up to provide gainful employment to people living in and around the forest."

It is not suggested that the modern man should return to the level of tribal people. Nor it is suggested that there should be immediate transplantation of the tribal people into the mainstream of modern society. The process of fusion is necessary but it has to be slow and steady without destroying the identity, culture and tradition of the tribes by improving their living conditions in their natural habitat. The judiciary in India has also shown its concern for the protection of rights of the tribals and at the same time protected the forests and allowed the development plans. (Jaswa, 2002).

The Supreme Court of India acknowledged by observing that it is common knowledge that *Adivasis* and other backward people living with the jungle had been using jungles around for collecting the requirement such as fruits, vegetables, fodder, flower, timber, animals and fuel-wood for their livelihood. The Supreme Court in this case gave detailed directions safeguarding and protecting the interests of the Adivasis and backward people who were being ousted from their forest land by National Thermal Power Corporation Ltd. (*A.I.R.1987*)

In my own experience it can be declared that the practical difficulties can be experienced with dedicated spirit otherwise blaming to the Government or the officer will create another disturbance. The Parlakhemundi-Koinpur-Tumba-Chikiti, the shortest route from Brahmapur to Parlakhemundi, and the work was started in 1962 and till now it is not yet completed. Lack of frequent inspection the medicinal herbs and other forest commodities are being exploited. No satisfactory education can be achieved in comparison with the headquarters' schools. Orissa formed in 1936 and Andhra Pradesh in 1954. During this period no visit was done to this area for supervision. Due to lack of communication, the result of which the demarcation line rocks were removed and dislocated by the land holders, the result of which boundary line of the state has already been disturbed.

It is said agriculture is the mother of all cultures. Communication net works can improver the economic condition of rural people, both culture and agriculture. Hence the roads are the main infrastructure to uplift the rural development.

REFERENCES

1. P.S. Jaiswal and Nishta Jaiswal, 1998, *Environmental Law,* with ref. to A.I.R., 1987, Supreme Court, Vol. 374.
2. Bohidar, R.N., *I.T.D.A, Souvenir*, Parlakhemundi, May 1983.
3. Brahman, M., and H.O. Saxena, Scientist Regional Research Laboratory, Bhubaneswar, Mahendragiri the Pride of Eastern Ghat, Pub OES BBSR 1993.
4. Jaiswal and Jaiswal, *Environmental Law*. New Delhi, 1998.
5. Maltby, T.J.Ed. (1918) *Ganjam District Manual.*
6. Patro S.N.Orissa Environmental Society, 1993, *Mahendragiri the Pride of Eastern Ghat,* Bhubaneswar.
7. Panda, K.V.N., 1983, *I.T.D.A. Souvenir* p. 46. Article Land Records and Settlement Operation in Ganjam Agency.
8. Pani, Rabi Narayan, Ganjam 1990, the 8th 5 Year Plan in Ganjam District.
9. Patro S.N., and Panda, G.K., 1994. *Environment, Resource and Development* Orissa Environmental Society, Bhubaneswar.
10. Pattnaik, N., *(1983) ITDA Souvenir*, Parlakhemundi.
11. Pattnaik, N., *(1984) I.T.D.A. Report*, Parlakhemundi.
12. Rao, M.S., 1994, *I.T.D.A Souvenir,* Parlakhemundi.
13. Thurston, E., 1913, *Provincial Geography of India.* Madras Museum. p. 21.
14. Orissa District Gazetteers, Ganjam, By Shri Nrusinha Charan Behuria, I.A.S. (retd.) Govt of Orissa 1992, pp. 565 & 619.
15. Orissa District Gazetteers, Ganjam, pp. 396, 399.
16. Census of India 2001.
17. Dr. Sarat Chandra Behera, Rise and Fall of the Sailodvhavas, p. 18.

4

Surface Transports in Orissa

A Look

Dr. R.N.Misra*
Rookesh Kumar Misra**

For achieving rapid economic development of the state as well as country surface transport plays a vital role in this present world. The ongoing economic reforms therefore attach high priority to development of transport. Development of transportation infrastructure is also essential for marketing of agricultural products and enabling the farmers to get a fair price. Surface transport, not only help for the agricultural development of the country but also it help for the development of industry as well as service sector. All-weather connectivity to every village is necessary for improving the quality of life and economic condition in rural area. For the development of rural economy, roads are considered as basic need and need high priority. So, Government of India launched Pradhan Mantri Gram Sadak Yojana (PMGSY) in the year 2000 to provide connectivity by way of an all-weather road with necessary culverts and cross-drainage structures to the unconnected habitations in the rural area in such a way that habitations with a population of 1000 persons and above are connected in three years and all unconnected habitations with a population of 500 persons and above by the end of the Tenth Plan Period (2007)

* **Dr. Misra, Professor in MBA, SMIT, Ankushpur, Berhampur (Orissa).**

** **Mr. Misra is a Research Scholar.**

Roads in the State of Orissa

In absence of adequate rail linkages, roads are the major means of transportation in the state. The total road length in the state of Orissa was 2,38,006 kms. as on 31.03.2004. The detail is explained in Table 4.1.

As per the Table 4.1, the different categories of roads of the state was 2,38,006, kms. as on 31.03.2004. According to 2001 census, the population of the state is 368.05 lakh, this means, for 368 people only 2 kms. roads are available even after 60 years of independence of the country.

Table 4.1: Details of the Roads of Orissa as on 31.03.2004

(in Km.)

Sl.No.	*Particulars*	*Length of the Road*
1.	National Highway	3,193
2.	State Expressways	30
3.	State Highway	5,102
4.	Major District Roads	3,189
5.	Other District Roads	6,122
6.	Panchayat Samiti Roads	20,324
7.	Rural Roads	28,305
8.	Gram Panchayat Roads	1,39,942
9.	Forest Roads	7,242
10.	Urban Roads	18,132
11.	Irrigation Roads	6,277
12.	GRIDCO Roads	88
	Total	**2,38,006**

Source: Economic Survey, 2004-05, p-12/1.

National Highways of the State

National Highways of the state are explained in the Table 4.2.

Table 4.2: National Highways of the state

(in Km.)

Sl. No.	Date	No.of N.H.	District Covered	Total Length
1.	31.03.2003	12	25	3193
2.	31.03.2004	12	25	3193
3.	31.03.2005	12	25	3512

Source: Economic Survey of Orissa.

There is no progress in National Highway of the state in the year 2005 just 319 kms. road has increased from the year 2003 which is very insignificant.

Motor Vehicles Position of the State

Though there is no significant development in the length of road, but motor vehicles (both private and Government) has been increased. The Table 4.3 indicate the total vehicles of the state.

Table 4.3: Motor vehicles of road in Orissa

Sl. No.	Type of Vehicles	No. of Vehicles as on March				% increase over 2002-2003
		2001	2002	2003	2004	
1.	Goods Vehicle	67,743	77,147	84,268	94,859	12.6
2.	Public/Private Bus	4,499	4,787	4,946	5,297	7.1
3.	Motor car/Jeep/ Taxi	51,979	58,670	66,691	80,510	20.7
4.	Auto Rickshaw	6,187	8,787	11,310	15,068	33.4
5.	Motor Cycle/ Scooter, Mopeds	7,35,742	8,26,548	9,43,178	10,64,323	12.8
6.	Others	9.217	10,616	10,677	11,789	10.4
	Total	8,75,367	9,86,555	11,21,070	12,71,864	13.45

Source: Economic Survey, 2004-2005, p-12/6.

From the Table 4.3 it reveals that during four years, from 2001 to 2004, 50 per cent growth have been indicated. For 31 person one motor vehicle has been used by the person of State of Orissa.

The percentage of annual growth and average vehicles used for the person of the state is indicated in the table 4.4

From the Table 4.4 it is clear that in year 1990 per lakh population there are only nine buses, but the same has increased to 14 buses during the year 2004. Similarly 17 buses were used in the year 1990 on the basis of 1000 sq. kms. and same has increased to 34 buses during the year 2004.

Table 4.4: The percentage annual growth/average growth of motor vehicles from 1990 to 2004

Year	*Percentage of annual growth*	*No.of buses per lakh population*	*No.of buses per 1000 sq.kms.*	*No.of goods vehicles per lakh population*
1990	15.02	9	17	83
1995	16.69	11	24	112
2000	12.15	12	28	166
2002	12.70	13	31	210
2003	13.63	13	32	230
2005	13.45	14	34	258

Source: Economic Survey, Orissa (Ann 12.2).

The different categories of motor vehicles on the road in Orissa from the year 1990 to 2004 are explained in the Table 4.5.

Table 4.5: Different categories of vehicles of road in Orissa

Year as on March	*No.of buses*	*Goods vehicles*	*Car/Taxi jeeps*	*Motor cycles/ mopeds*	*Thee wheelers*	*Others*	*Total*
1990	2714	25,825	22,544	2,07,293	813	1213	2,60,402
1995	3681	37,822	31,807	3,70,974	2,281	4,876	4,51,441
2000	4372	60,059	45,660	6,54,114	5,561	9,025	7,78,781
2001	4499	67,743	51,797	7,35,742	6,187	9217	8,75,367
2002	4787	77,147	58,670	8,26,548	8,787	10,616	9,86,555
2003	4946	84,268	66,691	9,43,176	11,310	10,677	11,21,070
2004	5297	98,859	89,510	10,06,4323	15,086	11,789	12,71,864

Source: Economic Survey, 2004-2005, P-ANX -44.

The Table 4.5 reveals that the total motor vehicles on road were 260402 in the year 1990, which means one vehicle is available for 158 persons. But in the year 2004 the number of vehicles on the road has increased to 12,71,864 which means one vehicle available for 36 persons.

Rail Transport

Orissa has so far remained backward in the field of development of railways. The existing railway lines pass through the fringes of the state leaving the central areas untouched. This inadequacy is one of the factors which has an adverse impact on the pace of infrastructural and industrial development in the state. The state had 2,287 kms. of railway routes including 91 kms. of narrow gauge as on 31.03.2004. The railways route length in the state per thousand square kilometer of area comes to 14.7 kms. By 2002-03 a length of 552 kms. was electrified. There are 234 railway stations and 27 passenger halts in the state during 2003-04. The railway routes covers all the districts of the state expect seven districts i.e. Boudh, Deogarh, Kandhamal, Kendrapara, Malkangiri, Nawarangpur and Naryagarh.

The State Government has been pursuing proposals relating to the expansion of the railway network in the state through the Rail Coordination Directorate which is functioning under the administrative control of the Transport Department. The Directorate also functions as a liaisoning agency between the State Government and Railway Authorities for development of rail communication and movement of freight and essential commodities. A new railway zone namely East Coast Railway has been formed with three railway divisions namely Khurda Road, Waltair and Sambalpur and become fully operational with effect from the 1st April 2003. The headquarter of newly formed Railway Zone is located at Bhubaneswar.

5

Role of Surface Transport in Rural Development

A Case Study of Phulbani District

Dr. Pradeep Pattanayak*

Being a large country India has one of the largest road network in the World. The Ninth Five Year Plan laid emphasis on a co-ordinated and balanced road network throughout the length and breadth of the country. The primary road system covers National Highways. The Central Government is responsible for the National Highway system. The secondary and feeder road system covers state highway and major district roads. The third category are the rural roads and other district roads substantial outlays, were proposed for development in the rural and tribal areas.

Road transport is the second important mode of transport in India. It covers every corner of the country, which the railway transport even could not cover. Road transport provide the basic infrastructural facilities to both the agricultural and industrial sector of the country, moreover construction and maintenance of roads can generate huge employment opportunities.

In India, total length of roads has increased from 4 lakh kms. in 1950-51 to nearly 33.19 lakh kms in 1996-97, out of which 15.2 lakh kms is surfaced and the rest 18.01 kms. is unsurfaced. This shows that annual growth rate of this increase in road length was

* **Lecturer in Economics & Director (CSSRS), K.D. Science College, Pochilima,(Ganjam).**

4.5 per cent. National Highways, which have a total length is nearly 34,500 kms., constitute only 2 per cent of the total road system of the country. About 64 per cent of the villages of the country have a rural road network and the rest 36 per cent have no road connection. Moreover, over 65 per cent of our villages do not have any all weather roads.

At present, India has a total road network covering 2.88 million kms., which makes it the third largest road network in the world. It is estimated that road traffic in India accounts for 80 per cent of passenger traffic and 60 per cent of goods traffic in the country. Again, the projected figure shows, that by the year 2000, 85 per cent of the passengers traffic and 65 per cent of the goods traffic will be met through road transport system.

In our Five Year Plans, a good amount of fund was allocated for the development of roads. During the first three Plans and the Annual Plans, nearly Rs. 1,104 crores was spent on the heads of road development, again the fourth, fifith, sixth and seventh plan allocated funds worth Rs. 562 crores, Rs. 1348 crores, Rs. 3439 crores, and Rs 5,200 crores respectively for the development of roads in the country.

An outlay of Rs. 593 crores has been approved for the central sector roads in 1993-94, which includes a provision of Rs. 569.99 crores for National Highways. Enabling measures to permit the private sector to invest and fund development of National Highway work will be initiated in this year. An outlay of Rs, 2155.59 corers has been approved for road development in the states and the U.T. for Annual Plan 1993-94.

The Rakesh Mohan Committee on infrastructure development has recommended following measures to improve the highway infrastructure. The funds required for highway infrastructure development is of the order of Rs. 3,200 crores from 1996-97 to 2001-02 and an additional amount of Rs. 63,000 crores shall be needed between 2001-02 and 2005-06, all sources—public, private domestic and foreign would have to be trapped. In this scheme of financing the government is still required to be a major player, other sources identified by the panel for 1996-2001 were private sector (Rs. 10,000 crores) multilateral and bilateral lending agencies (Rs. 4000 crores) and total collections (Rs.2,000 crores)

On an average National Highway Authority of India will deliver more then 1000 kms. of upgraded four lanes National Highway every year over next 10 years. It will be the proposed and mandated are totalled up, then a phenomenal sum of Rs. 80,000 crores shall be needed to build about 14,000 kms. of 4 lane 5,200 kms., of widening to 2 lanes, 1,500 kms. of strengthening existing 2 lane National Highways. This amount includes the building of 470 bridges, construction of 40 bypasses and also to build some 2000 kms. of expressways.

Road Transport System in India

In India road transport system is rendering a valuable service to the general people in various directions of their life. Road transport in India may be classified as traditional and mechanized transport traditional transport includes non-mechanized transport like bullock carts, thetas, rickshaws etc. About 25 per cent of India's trade is carried through this traditional mode of transport, which directly employed nearly 2 crores of people. Further, mechanized road transport includes all those transport facilities carried through motor vehicles whose number are increasing at a very fast rate, Total number of vehicles on road has increased from 0.3 million in 1950-51 to 37.2 million on 1996-97 .Total number of buses has gone up from 34,000 to 4,88,000 and total number of trucks has increased from 82,000 to 22,60,000 during the above-mentioned period. Thus, the annual rate of growth of this transport was 5.4 per cent. At present, there are 66 State Road Transport Undertakings. Which have a total fleet of over 1.2 lakh, buses on March 1993 carrying 6.8 crores passengers daily. Moreover, to develop Inter-State route, a Transport Development Council and Inter-State Transport Commission were established. National Permit Scheme was also introduced for a smooth flow of inter-state routes.

Demographic Profile of Orissa

The total population of Orissa as on March 2001 was 36,706,920 according to the provisional census 2001 with a decadal growth rate of 15.94 per cent. Which is lower than the decadal growth rate of India (21.34%). This Constitutes 3.57 per cent of total population of India as per 2001 Census. 3.5 per cent of population of Orissa resides in an area of 155,707 sq. kms. As per 2001 Census, the sex ratio female per 1000 male was 972 and 971 in 1991 Census. There are also variation in sex ratio in different district of Orissa. Gajapati district has recorded the highest sex ratio of 1031 in 2001 census. The lowest sex ratio of 901 has been observed in the district of Khurda in the state of Orissa.

Road Transport Service in Orissa

In the absence of adequate internal rail linkages roads are the major means of transportation in the state. The total road length in the state of Orissa was 2,18,626 kms. as on 31.3 1997 of which 23. 30 per cent are surfaced as against 2,18,395 kms. during 1995-96. The total road length and surfaced road per 100sq. kms. of area amounted to 31.0 kms. and 12.20 kms. as compared to the all India average of 42.0 kms. and 29.3 kms. The length of different categories of roads in the State including 1625 kms. of National Highway, 67 kms. of Express Highway, 4906 kms. of State Highway, 4735 kms. of M.D.R., 4750 kms. of O.D.R, 4670 kms. of C.V.R., 14,303 kms. of village roads 20,427 kms. of Panchayat Samiti Roads. 1,39,968 kms. of G.P. roads, 7030 kms. of forest roads, 10280 kms. of Municipal roads, 6277 kms. of irrigation roads, and 88 kms of O.S.E.B. (Gridco) roads in the state of Orissa.

All weather connectivity to every village is necessary prerequisite for improving the quality of life and economic conditions in rural areas. At the end of 1991-92, 5 Sub Divisional headquarters' and 9 Block headquarters were lacking all weather connectivity to their districts and Sub-Divisional headquarters respectively 3 such Sub-Divisional headquarters and 5 such Block headquarters have been connected to concerned district and Sub-Divisional head quarters respectively by the end of 1996-97 construction of bridges to connect the remaining 2 sub-divisions and 4 Blocks are under progress and are expected to be completed soon. Rural Connectivity has been identified as one of the basic minimum services for development of agriculture as well as rural development for which the State Government of Orissa has accorded priority attention to this sector. During 1996-97 an amount of Rs. 44.02 crore was provided to the Rural Development Department for Construction of bridges and development of roads. 60 bridges, 205 kms. of black-topped roads 300 kms. of metal roads were constructed and all weather connectivity to 315 villages were provided alongwith generation of 63 lakh Mandays during 1996-97 out of 46992 inhabited villages in the state, all weather connectivity to 18649 villages (40%) have been provided by the end of 1996-97. Provisions of funds to the tune of Rs. 48.00 crore has been made. During 1997-98 and it had been targeted to complete the construction of 50 on-going bridges 260 kms. of black topped roads 600 kms., of metalled roads, 652 kms. of morum roads and to connect 100 villages to their G.P headquarters with all weather roads.

The detailed road length service in the State of Orissa has been depicted in the Table 5.1. (*See on pages 42, 43*).

Demographic Profile of Phulbani (Kandhamal) District

Phulbani (kandhamal) district is one of lowest density populated district next to Malakanagiri district of Orissa. In addition to the total population is also lowest in the district among 30 districts of Orissa except Malakanagiri, Nuapada, Boudh and Deogarh district. The geographical land area of the district is approximataly 8021 sq. kms The phulbani district has a total population of 6,48,000 lakhs. According to 2001 Census, which constitutes 1.76 per cent of the total population in the state. The decadal growth rate of district population indicates 18.66 per cent as on 2001 census. The share of male population in the total was 3,23,000 lakhs and the female population in the total was 3,25,000 lakhs as on 2001 Census in the Phulbani district. According to 2001 Census the sex ratio shows that 1068 females for 1000 males. The district has fourth position in sex ratio in the State as on 2001 census.The literacy rate is 52.68 per cent and the male and female literacy rates is 69.79 per cent and 35.86 per cent respectively. The Schedule Caste and Schedule Tribe population is 1,09,506 lakhs and 3,36,809 lakhs respectively having 71 per cent in both community to total population of the district as on 2001 Census. The percentage of rural population to total population of the district is approximately 93.20 per cent as on 2001 census. The percentage of rural population to total population of the district is approximately 93.20 per cent as on 2001 Census.

The Phulbani district comprises of 2 Sub-Division viz. Phulbani and Balliguda, 4 Tahasils, 12 Community Development Blocks, 15 Police Stations, 153 Gram Panchayats alongwith 2546 total village. There are no municipality only two towns and one NAC in a rural based tribal and underdeveloped district.

Table 5.1: Different categories of road length (in kms.) as on 01.06.2003

Sl. No.	Districts	National Highway (03-04)	Express Highway (03-04)	State Highway (03-04)	Major District Roads (03-04)	Other District Roads (03-04)	Rural Roads (03-04)	G.P Roads (03-04)	Panchayat Samiti Roads (03-04)	Forest Roads (03-04)	Railway Route length	No.of Railway stations (in kms.) (03-04)
1	2	3	4	5	6	7	8	9	10	11	12	13
1.	Angugul	256		182	-	356	687	7302	764	431	103	10
2.	Balasore	118		67	105	326	1221	1682	787	59	115	18
3.	Buragarh	98		142	113	135	1112	6560	1303	231	53	3
4.	Bhudrak	40		117	122	90	863	1572	476		28	4
5.	Bloangir	139		140	126	300	1228	5827	878	251	177	14
6.	Boudh	-		228	-	29	502	3745	173	229	-	-
7.	Cattack	64		202	129	381	1275	2641	814	192	114	15
8.	Deogarh	190		32	4	16	663	2891	289	116	-	
9.	Dhinkanal	131		17	105	242	805	5670	628	226	51	5
10.	Gajapati	-		250	66	39	479	4253	301	107	49	7
11.	Ganjam	212		623	92	481	2338	6717	761	480	86	9
12.	Jagatashingpur	10		109	41	191	807	1308	673	1	70	7
13.	Jaipur	154	20	61	72	319	970	2656	792	36	99	10
14.	Jharusuguda	106		27	-	33	479	2850	348	23	84	8

(Table 5.1 Contd...)

1	2	3	4	5	6	7	8	9	10	11	12	13
15.	Kalahandi	184		215	266	46	1061	9955	517	308	38	5
16.	Kandhamal (Phulbani)	144		321	78	209	775	5651	532	357	-	-
17.	Kendrapada	45		63	50	328	744	2512	684	20	-	-
18.	Keonjhar	273	9	111	78	359	1229	2435	926	252	58	6
19.	Khurda	112		18	505	182	923	4925	595	236	118	14
20.	Koraput	174		213	209	242	778	4973	986	217	234	20
21.	Malkangiri	-		252	54	56	824	2954	357	98	-	
22.	Mayurbhanj	193		327	156	447	2466	6641	1383	986	99	12
23.	Nawrengapur	42		122	-	-	1019	5127	1305	292	-	-
24.	Nayagarh	9		51	125	235	545	5497	506	335	-	-
25.	Nuapada	93		40	52	233	262	4133	504	113	32	3
26.	Puri	49		158	85	287	796	7282	574	19	42	6
27.	Rayagada	-		391	130	69	931	4032	751	198	117	10
28.	Sambalpur	207		183	62	138	904	6499	603	734	168	17
29.	Sonepur	13		79	59	49	385	3032	313	42	13	1
30.	Sundargarh	168		218	296	274	1294	8620	801	673	339	30
	Orissa	**3194**	**29**	**4959**	**3180**	**6092**	**28365**	**139942**	**20324**	**7267**	**2237**	**234**

Source: Districts at a Glance, 2005, Orissa, Directorate of Eco & Statistics, Bhubaneswar.

Rural Transport Services in Phulbani (Kandhamal) District

The road (Surface) transport services in the Phulbani (Kandhamal) district through network of National Highway is 114 kms., State Highway is 321 kms. Major district road is 78 kms. Other district road is 209 kms., Rural road is 775 kms. G.P. roads is 5651 Kms, Panchayat Samiti road is 357 kms. Railway route is zero (Nil) Kms. for the district population upto in the year 2003-04.

The most crucial problem in the Phulbani district railway network service facilities is very poor compared to other districts of the State. Now, six districts viz. Boudha, Deogharh, Kendrapada. Nawarangpur and Nuapada including of Phulbani (Kandhamal) district in the state of Orissa, which is under, minimize to other efforts towards socio-economic development of the district. The people of Phulbani district are deprived from railway service and depended to only Berhampur and Muniguda (Rayagada) railway station, which is far away i.e. 170 kms from the Phulbani district. Under these circumstances the importance of launching the railway service network in a mass-scale needs no emphasis. Similarly, Daringabadi is a famous hilly station and Chakapada is a historical place in Phulbani district. That is, far away approximately 100 kms. distance from the district headquarters. The important tourist place are suitable point of view. The village and a few numbers of G.P. road is very weak muddy and unsurfaced road and connectivity to the hilly and remote sense area in the Phulbani district. A large number of village roads are underdeveloped and backward in such a tribal district. The road service network of rural area in the district is very miserable condition. There is no such type of large scale industry and declared as a zero industry zone in the district

The detailed road (surface) transport and communication service network in the Phulbani district is depicted in the Table 5.2.

Table 5.2: Length of different categories of roads in Phulbani district (in kms.)

Sl. No.	Categories of Roads	Years				
		1999-2000	2000-2001	2001-2002	2002-2003	2003-2004
1.	National Highway	-	-	121	121	114
2.	State Highway	340	289	325	325	321
3.	Major District Roads	182	133	78	78	78
4.	Other District Roads	63	63	150	150	209
5.	Rural Roads/Village Roads	279+682	279+853	133+627	-	775
6.	G.P.Roads	5651	5651	5650	5650	5651
7.	Panchyat Samiti Roads	-	532	532	532	532
8.	Forest Roads	323	323	358	358	357
9.	Railway Route Length	Nil	Nil	Nil	Nil	Nil
10.	No. of Railway Stations	Nil	Nil	Nil	Nil	Nil

Source: District Statistical Hand Book, Phulbani. Directorate of Eco & Stat. Bhubanswer.

Suggestions

The tribal people are very backward, primitive nature with living below standard and deprived from the fundamental right and needs of the nation. The tribal people of Phulbani district are deprived in whole point of view, such as, socio-economic, culture and other necessary developmental activities owing to weaker road (surface) transport network service. Similarly, the populations of the district are also far away from railway transport service after 60 years of independence of the country. Railway transport service is a dream for the people of the district. They are waiting for a golden sunshine of a good morning day due to the on-going common problem. They are also backward in education, health, industry, employment and entertainment service as well as in every respect since in a long years. The following suggestions may adopt in government policy in the aforesaid problem for the development of all weather road and railway service in the tribal and backward district are mentioned below:

1. To proper identify the hilly and remote sense area as a tourist place in the district and it will be well connected to National Highway and State Highway;
2. To make and adopt a strong and suitable plan by the Central Government for eradication of the surface and railway transport problem;
3. To establish the purposed Khurda-Bolangiri railway route through the district;
4. To establish large scale industry based on minor forest produce goods, Medicinal plants, garden and zoological park and botanical garden in the district;
5. To attract and invite the foreign and domestic tourist to different tourist spots, for to establish eco-tourism industry in the district;
6. To declare a specially backward zone in industry and railway service and add in to in the K.B.K. central programme;
7. To keep more funds (capital) in Central budget for the development of surface road and railway route network in the district.

REFERENCES

1. *The Employment News*, Vol. XXVII, No-10, 8-14 June 2002.
2. *Annual Plan, 1993-94*, Govt. of India, Planning Commission, New Delhi.
3. *Economic Survey (Orrisa)*, 1997-98, Directorate of Eco. and Stat. Bhubaneswar.
4. *District Statistical Hand Book (Phulbani)*, Directorate of Eco. and Stat. Bhbaneswar.
5. *Districts at a Galance, 2005 (Phulbani)*, Bureau of Eco. and Stat. Bhubaneswar.
6. Indian Economy,P.K. Dhar, 2000 *Kalyani Publication*, New Delhi.

6

Management of Surface Transport in India

A Look

Dr. Anil Kumar Sahu*
Dr. R.N. Misra**

Introduction

India is an immense land with immense diversity. It is the seventh largest nation by area and the second by pupulation. It is the world's largest democracy and is the birth place to many of the world's religions. It has more millionaires than Australia has people. It is often described as a third world nation, yet it has some of the world's most sophisticated technology. People live on the street and people live in mansions. Daily ox carts pull loads of supplies through the capital city of Delhi and yet this country is a nuclear power. It is a truly diverse and amazing place—a world within one country. So too are India's transport systems; they accommodate a diverse range of transport tasks through a vastly different array of vehicle types. India shows considerable innovation and persistence; the transport system have the old and new, operating side by side.

Of India's 3.3 million kms. road network, 195,231 km (6%) are National and State Highways. Only two to three per cent of the

---

* **Dr. Sahu, Reader in MBA, Berhampur University, Bhanja Bihar (Orissa).**

** **Dr. Misra, Professor in MBA, S.M.I.T., Ankushpur, Berhampur (Orissa).**

network is four laned while 15 per cent is single laned. With India's 1 billion people, the 3.3 million kms. of roads carries 85 per cent of total passenger movements and 70 per cent of freight traffic, and creates a massive transport challenge for any country.

The key concepts in todays world-economy derive their very existence because of the physical and electronic linkages developed by the technology. There would be neither a world market nor globalization nor liberalization without the existence of reliable and robust means of transportation. In fact, in today's competitive market the prices are dicated to a large extent by the elements of logistics, e.g., long-haul transportation, local cartage, packaging, constitutes the basic linkage between the supply and demand centers. The 'demand' of transportation is a 'secondary demand' as against the 'primary demand' of the commodities and the consumables. There, it is very difficult to assess the 'demand' of transportation at a given time as the same depends upon a large number of unpredictable variables. Some of such variables may be enumerated as follows: The availability of the raw-materials, the seasonality of the product, the seasonality of the demand, the quantitative volume of the requirement, distance between the supply and demand centers, competition between the various available modes of transportation, etc.

There are certain characteristics which are perculiar to the transportation industry. There are extremely sharp peaks and troughs in the demand of transportation. As consequence, the transportation-infrastructure has to be geared up to meet the demand of the peaks. This necessarily leads to the idling of assets during the lean periods. The other feature is the "public" nature of the transport infrastructure. The capital costs involved in building of railways, roads, bridges, flyovers, jetteys and airports etc. is so high and returns so slow that the government involvement and financing through the public funds becomes essential. Only mobile assets such as trucks, ships, aeroplanes etc. can be financed by the private capital.

There is also a definite relationship between the nature of the individual commodities and the modes of transportation preferred by that commodity. For example, the commodities having bulk production and bulk demand with longer leads naturally prefer railways over the roads. The commodities having continuous production and seasonal demand require warehousing over long periods and such movements are preferable by the railways. Also in case of continuous production and continuous demand, if the volumes are in huge bulk, railways are a preferable mode of transport. The high-value, lighter, fragile and perishable commodities prefer road rail for their transport.

The various modes of transportation used for bulk freight traffic are rail, road, coastal and high-seas shipping, inland waterways, pipelines and ropeways. The energy efficiency and the pollution factors are becoming more and more relevant in today's transport economics. In the coming days of the "green transport" the railways and the coastal and inland water transport are bound to become more and more dominant.

In India, over the years more and more inland freight traffic has been shifting from rail to road. In the year 1951 about 88 per cent of country's freight was moving on rail and 10 per cent on roads. But the situation has changed drastically over the last few decades and today about 60 per cent of the freight moves on the road and about 38 per cent on railways. The protential of the coastal and inland water transportation is yet to be exploited in a significant way in our country.

Road Transportation

The advantage of road transport include door to door service, greater operational flexibility, negotiable rates, personalized service, less stringent packaging norms, economic movement in smaller lots etc the transportation by road reduces the number of intermediate handlings and consequent damages. It is also more amenable to just-in-time concept of the inventory control.

Total length of Indian roads in about 3 million kms. out of which 52000 kms are the prime arterial routes called National Highways (NH). The NHs carry about 40 per cent of the freight traffic. The NHs are under the overall responsibility of a Central Govt. body called the National Highways Authority of India (NHAI). Its plan includes provision of 4 to 6 land highways connecting the four metropolis cities. This would require upgradation of about 15000 kms. of highways with an estimated expenditure of Rs. 20,000 crore (1 crore = 10 million). In addition to adopting other means of resource-mobilization, an additional surcharge Re.1 per litre is being levied on petrol w.e.f. June 1998. The participation of the private sector is also being encouraged through the BOT (Build-Operate-Transfer) schemes and some important road segments are coming up on this pattern. The main law controlling the road transportation in India is the Motor Vehicles Act of 1939 which deals with the aspects of registration vehicles, driving lincences, fitness certificates, pollution control, safety regulations, loadability conditions, precautions for carriage of hazardous commodities etc. The main constraints for road transport are poor riding quality of roads, weak and narrow culverts and bridges with insufficient clearance for movement of higher dimensional vehicles and the octroi and check posts. There are about 22 lakhs heavy duty and 6 lakhs high duty trucks in the country. The normal permissible axle loads are 9-10 tonnes. The road trucking is almost completely in the private sector.

Rail Transport

The Indian Railways are one of the largest Railway system in the world. This network consists of more than 7000 Railway Stations with a track age of about 1,08,000 kms. covering a route of about 63,000 kms. The Indian Railways run 11,000 trains per day. This railway system carries about 441 million tonnes of goods traffic and 4410 million passengers-journey per year. Today more than 95 per cent of its freight traffic is limited to 8-9 bulk commodities such as coal, POL, raw materials, iron & steel. Foodgrains, fertilizers, sugar, cement, etc. The freight rates are decided on the principles of the ability of a commodity to pay. Thus, the freight rates for salt, foodgrains and ferilizers are cheaper than those for coal, POL, cement, steel etc. This system is called the classification of freight rates.

To achieve the modernization of the Railway system, the main trusst-areas have been identified as: (i) The policy of uni-gauge, (ii) Electrification, (iii) Upgradation of tracks & bridges, (iv) Electronic communication and signaling; and (v) High speed-high loadability wagons and other rolling stocks.The freight rates and passenger fares of 5/- the Railways are controlled by the parliament through a separate Railways Budget. Despite these controls and public obligations the Indian Railways are running on self generated revenue and are also making a profit. This is quite creditable when compared with the world-wide decline of the Railway system particularly in the more advanced countries. The Railways are also inviting participation of private capital through their BOLT, Own your Wagon Schemes, and the Railway Bonds.

The key operating strategy of the Indian Railways has been to encourage long lead bulk movement in full train loads called 'rakes'. To achieve this the Railways have already replaced steam engines with diesel and electric locomotives. The old type of wagons having vacuum braking, screw-coupling, conventional bearings are being replaced with those having pneumatic (single or double pipe) air brakes, centre buffer coupling and roller bearing stocks. Now as a policy, only eight-wheeler bogie wagons are being used by IR and the older four-wheelers are being taken off the rails. This strategy permits higher throughput without incurring much cost on the permanent way infrastructure. The air braking permits higher speeds and CBC coupler permits packing of more tonnage in a rake. The roller bearing permits longer runs of a train without tonnage in a rake. The roller bearing permits longer runs of a train without enroute examination of the undergears. This has also obviated the need of huge MT), BCX (55.5 MT), BCN (58 MT), BCNA (58.8 MT), BOXNA (52 to 56+ 2 MT), BTPN (45 to 47 MT/66 to 67 Kilo Litre) and TP (4 Wheeler) 19 to 29 Kilo Litre).

The main constraints of the Indian Railway system are: (1) Congested bottleneck routes; (2) congested terminals; (3) Bad condition of rake handling terminals— No paved circulating area for trucks, no lighting, not enough covered sheds, no full rake length siding; (4) Shortage of covered wagons; (5) No user friendly rules and attitudes; and (6) Transit hazards due to pilferage etc. The action plan to remove these bottlenecks includes such strategies as: (1) Own your Wagon Scheme; (2) Engine on Load Scheme; (3) Long-haul trains; (4) High powered Locos; (5) Electrification; and (6) Gauge conversion/doubling.

REFERENCES

1. Dhingra, I.C., Indian Economy, *S.Chand and Sons*, New Delhi, 2004.
2. BT: *Business Today*, 1998, Competitiveness and Micro-Economics, September 22: pp. 96-101.

3. *World Bank*, India, Transport Sector Long Term Issue, Report March, 1995.
4. Narain Yogendra, New Initiatives in Infrastructure Sector, *Yojana*, January 1998, pp. 5.
5. *Economic Survey*, Government of India, 2002-03.

7

Transport and Economic Development in Orissa

Pradip K. Brahma
R.P. Sharma

Transport and communication are two of the important infrastructures for the economic development. Growth of agriculture, manufacturing, trade, commerce and banking are essential for economic prosperity but these sectors cannot be accelerated without the development of transportation. Without the efficient facilities for the movement of goods and people economic and social activities cannot be developed in the society.

There is a good correlation between the growth of road transport vehicles and economic development of a region. Of course, it is difficult to conclude that the growth of transport instigates the pace of the economic development or it is vice-versa. It also has been found that (Owen, 1989) immobility and poverty go together. The mobility index of freight and passengers remains within single digit in the economies of low per capita GNP. In the economies of higher per capita income the mobility index remain significantly high. A study shows (Economic Times, 1995) that in the Indian economy the economic growth of one per cent annually brings out about 1.2 to 1.4 per cent growth in transportation.

The progress of road transport can be measured through three indicators: (1) Growth (2) Density and (3) share in the total transport system.

Growth of Motor Vehicles: India has about 3 lakhs motor vehicles in 1950-51 and in about half a century it increased to gigantic figure of about 524 lakhs by the end of 2000 A.D. the growth rate was faster in the last decade of the twentieth century. In the year 1989-90 there were 170 lakh vehicles in the country which shows a three-fold increase by the end of the century. This comes to about 20.82 per cent annual growth rate in the nineties of 20th century.

Desity of Motor Vehicles: The desity of vehicles can be measured in two methods: (a) Motor vehicles per lakh of human population or (b) the number of motor vehicles per 100 kms. of surface roads. In the year 1950-51 the density was 85 vehicles per lakh of population of about 100 crores, this comes to about 4166 vehicles per lakh of population (Tata, 2002-03). By international standards this ratio is far from satisfactory.

Share of Road Transport: As far as the passenger traffic is concerned the road transport's share was about 26 per cent in the total road-railway transport system in the year 1950-51. This was increased to about 84 per cent by 2000 as a result of fast growth of passenger vehicle fleets in the private sector not only extended to the inter-state long distance routes but also extensive expansion of local transport with small vehicles.

Orissa Scenario

Orissa had 7.79 lakh vehicles of all categories for a population of 367 lakhs, which comes to 47 vehicles per lakh of population, as against 4166 in case of India. The motor vehicular density of Orissa is about 1.26 per cent of national figures. This indicates how Orissa is poorest in economic development. In per capita income (1999-2000 at current prices) Orissa is the last, state, with the exception of Bihar, with an annual per capita income of Rs. 9,162. This indicates also the poverty of the state which has 47.2 per cent of population below the poverty line as against only 6.2 per cent of people below the poverty line in Punjab. Of course in absolute terms, Uttar Pradesh has maximum number of people below the poverty line of 5.30 crores as against 1.69 crores of people in Orissa.

Inter-state Comparison

it is found that in six of the major states, the vehicle density is below the Indian average ratio which includes the state of Orissa. The other states are Assam, Bihar, Uttar Pradesh and West Bengal.

It is interesting to find that the Orissa ratio of 2,302 vehicles per lakh of population is above the states of Assam, Bihar and West Bengal. Punjab has the highest number of vehicles per lakh of population with 9.868 vehicles, flowed by Gujarat with 8,765 and Tamilnadu in the third position with 5,942 motor vehicles.

In the nineties of the last century Orissa made good progress in the growth of motor vehicles. In the year 1990 the total number of motor vehicles was 2.60 lakhs which increased to 7.79 lakhs by the end of the century. This shows that, in that decade the annual rate of growth of vehicles was around 19.96 per cent or about 20 per cent. In 1993-94 Orissa had 3.5 vehicles per square km.and 16.4 vehicles per thousand populations as against the all India averages of 8.3 and 30.5 respectively.

The growth rate of all vehicles in Orissa on annual basis is presented in Table 7.1. It shows that except in the year 1991 in which the growth rate was negative, in all the rest of the years the rates of growth ranged between 10.74 per cent (1996) and 19.27 per cent (1991), however the three year moving growth of the growth rate figures show that the growth rate of motor vehicles in the state is gradually moving in the downward trend. The growth of motor vehicles in absolute terms can be visualised from Fig. 7.1 presented in the form of bar diagrams.

Table 7.1: Growth of vehicles in Orissa, 1990-2000

Year	*Vehicles in lakhs*	*Annual growth per cent*	*Three year moving average growth, per cent*
1990	2.60	-	-
1991	3.10	19.27	-
1992	3.03	-2.16	9.56
1993	3.39	11.58	7.84
1994	3.36	14.10	14.12
1995	4.51	16.69	13.84
1996	4.99	10.74	13.34
1997	5.62	12.61	11.50
1998	6.25	11.15	11.58
1999	6.94	10.98	11.42
2000	7.78	12.15	-

Source: Economic Survey, Orissa, 2000-2001.

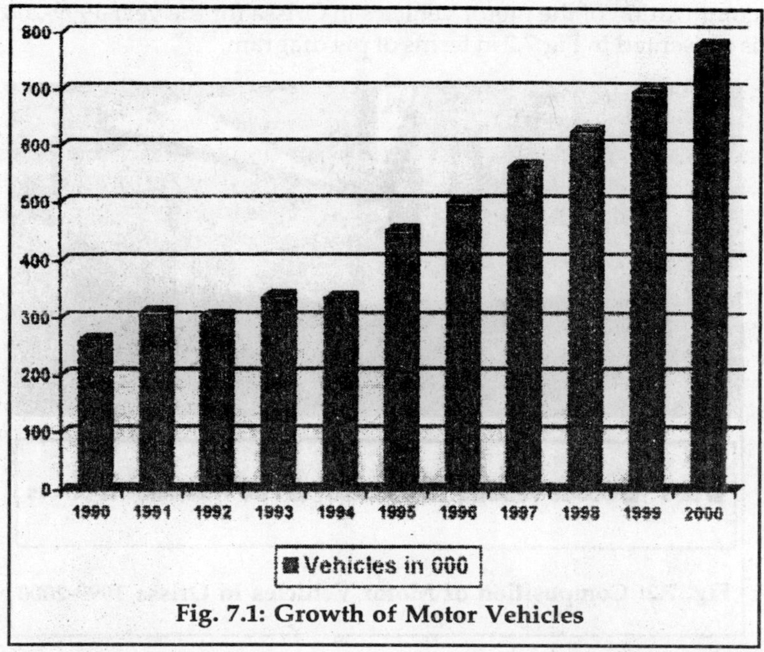

Fig. 7.1: Growth of Motor Vehicles

Composition of Motor Vehicles

Two-Wheelers: In the total number of motor vehicles the two wheelers are more prominent. In the total motor vehicles the two-wheelers forms 84.09 per cent in the year 1999-2000, but then years back it was 79.61 per cent. On the whole during the ten year period the growth rate of two wheels of motor bikes and scooters shown 215 per cent that is average growth rate of 21.5 per annum. Highest number of two wheelers is found in the two districts of Sundergar and Cuttack. Out of 6.80 lakhs two wheelers in the state 2.20 lakhs, which is about one-third of the motor bikes and scooters are found in these two districts.

Goods Vehicles: The growth of goods vehicles indicates the symptoms of economic activity and the growth of buses and stage carriages indicates the social development and increasing facilities of mobility among the people of the region. The goods vehicles formed about 8 per cent followed by cars and taxis of 6 per cent and the buses which are the vehicles of mass passenger transport forms about one per ent of the total vehicle in the 1999-2000. The composition of the motor vehicles in Orissa for the year 1999-2000 is presented in Fig.7.2 in terms of pie diagram.

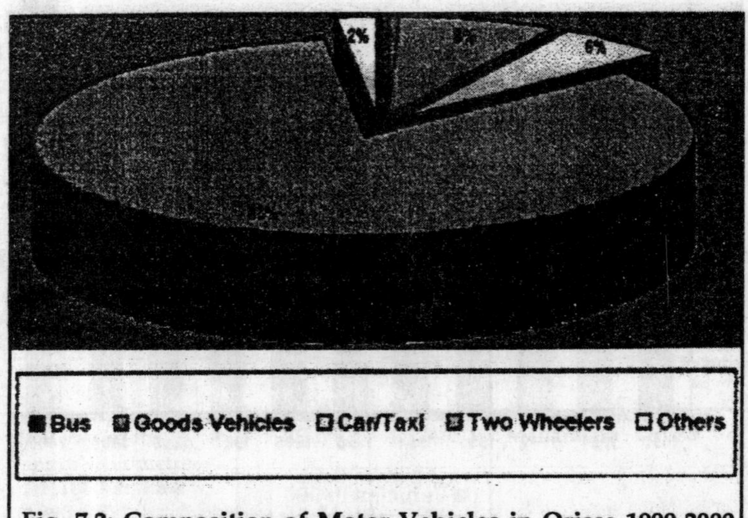

Fig. 7.2: Composition of Motor Vehicles in Orissa 1999-2000

Passenger Buses

The passenger buses formed only about one per cent of the total motor vehicles in Orissa. On an average there are 23.3 buses per lakh of population. The thirty districts of Orissa are divided into 17 transport zones and statistics of motor vehicles are available accordingly. After reorganisation of the districts the transport zones are not organised according to the revenue districts, hence 13 districts are merged with other newly formed districts as transport zones. In seven zones the bus per lakh of population is higher than the state average.

During the fifties of the last century the state transport system dominated the fleet of buses on the road but by the end of the century the state transport came to a deteriorated position. Even in 1995-96 the ORTC had a fleet strength of 836 buses of which 58.97 per cent were on the road. By 2000 the fleet strength dwindled to 615 of which 272 buses are on the road which constitutes about 44.22 per cent. The capital investment increased to Rs. 13.65 crore by the year 1999-2000 from that of Rs. 11.55 crores in 1995-96. On the other hand the buses on the road reduced by about 89.65 per cent over the above period. Presently out of the total number of 4,372 buses in the state the share of the ORTC comes to about 14.06 per cent.

The transport zone of Sambalpur (which included Deogarh and Jharsuguda revenue districts) has maximum number of passenger buses with 51.2 buses per lakh of population followed by Cuttack (includes Jagatsinghpur) with 47.5 buses per lakh of population and Sunsagarh in the third place with the ratio of 38.2 buses, in the lowest level Bargarh zone has 2.7 buses per lakh of population.

Of course, the zone-wise data of vehicles are not providing true picture of the passenger transport system available in the zones. This is because of the fact that the ownership and registration of the vehicles in a zone do not reflect the actual availability of bus routes in a zone. For instance even though maximum number of buses is found registered in Sambalpur but in fact the bus routes are extended widely in the neighbouring districts rather than in Sambalpur itself.

Buses, cars and other four-wheelers per lakh of population in different transport zones of Orissa is shown in Table 7.2. (*See on next page*).

Car and Other Four-Wheelers

Private cars and jeeps and other four-wheelers also indicate the economic activity and standard of living of a region. In the state as a whole there are 190 four-wheelers per lakh of population. In India car and jeeps constitute about 13.26 per cent of the total motor vehicles, in Orissa it is about 6 per cent.

In comparison to the national figures the car/jeeps and other four-wheelers taken together, there are 146 vehicles per lakh of population as against 190 vehicles in Orissa for the same ratio. Khurdha transport zone has the highest number of 628 cars because of capital city of Bhubaneswar where the official cars and jeeps are highest in number.

Table 7.2: Buses and cars per lakh of population-2000

No	District/ zone	Population lakhs	Bus per lakhs of population	Car/Jeeps per lakh of population
1.	Balasore	33.55	15.0	50
2.	Bargarh	13.46	2.7	23
3.	Bolangir	22.50	17.7	75
4.	Cuttack	33.98	47.7	489
5.	Dhenkanal	22.05	17.0	109
6.	Ganjam	36.54	16.7	75
7.	Jaipur	29.25	7.3	32
8.	Kalahandi	18.65	13.0	82
9.	Kandhamal	6.48	25.1	108
10.	Kendujhar	15.62	31.4	165
11.	Khurdha	27.38	29.5	628
12.	Koraput	26.76	23.2	109
13.	Mayurbhanj	22.22	22.6	75
14.	Puri	14.97	24.1	130
15.	Rayagada	8.23	5.9	20
16.	Sambalpur	17.12	51.2	341
17.	Sundargarh	18.29	38.2	482
	Orissa	**367.05**	**23.3**	**190**

Source: Economic Survey, Orissa, 2000-2001.

Cuttack is in second position with 489 cars per lakh of population and Sundargarh is in third position with 482 cars per lakh of population. The former district is a commercial capital of Orissa and the latter has the Rourkela Steel Plant in it which is the reason of high ratio of cars and jeeps. In rest of the 14 transport ones, 8 zones have four-wheelers numbering 75 or less per lakh of population.

Number of cars, jeep and other four-wheeler motor vehicles in the transport zones and the districts Orissa are presented in Fig. 7.3.

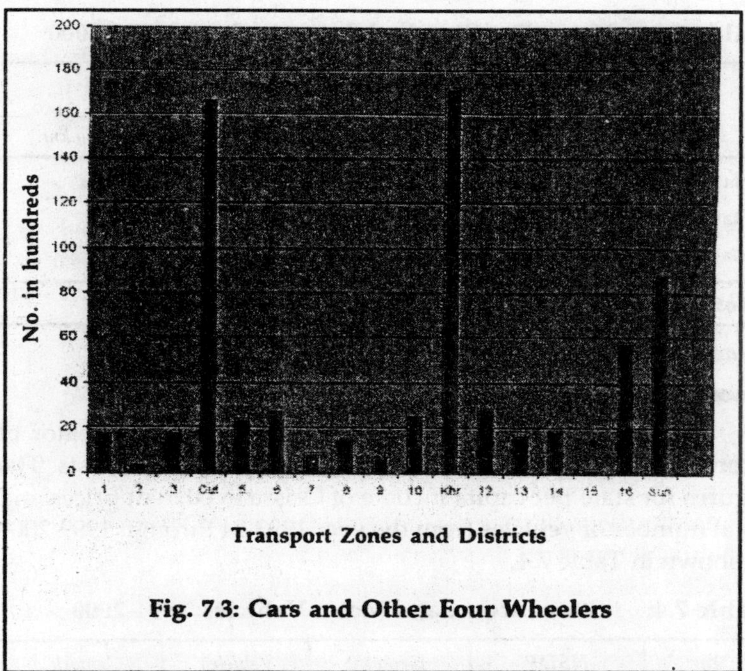

Fig. 7.3: Cars and Other Four Wheelers

Network of Roads

Growth of motor vehicles depends upon the good network of roads. The three categories of roads which are regarded as standard black top roads are, National Highways, State Highways and Major District Roads. These roads constitute only about 4.98 per cent of total of all types of roads. Of this the National Highways form 1.21 per cent .The rest of the roads, except the roads of urban areas, are village roads, forest roads etc. are not suitable for vehicular traffic and most of them are fair-weather roads which form about 95 per cent of the total road system of network in the state.

The length of standard roads in Orissa is presented in Table 7.3. It can be verified from the Table that the standard roads is 7 km per 100 sq.km. of area.

Table 7.3: Length of Standard Roads in Orissa 1999-2000

Type of Road	*Km*	*Per cent to Total Road Length*	*Road Length in km Per 100 Sq.km.*
National High way	2,752	1.21	1.7
State High Way	4,816	2.12	3.0
Major Dist. Roads	3,727	1.65	2.3
Total	**11,295**	**4.98**	**7.00**

Source: Economic Survey, Orissa. 2000-2001.

Economic Development and Motor Vehicles

Growth of per capita income is an important indicator of economic development usually accepted by the economists. The figures for state per capita income of Orissa in current prices and total number of vehicles from the year 1993-94 through 1999-2000 is shown in Table 7.4.

Table 7.4: State Income and Motor Vehicles: 1994-2000

Year	*NSDP per capita Rs. in 000*	*Growth per cent*	*Vehicles in lakhs*	*Growth per cent*
1993-94	4.79	-	3.36	-
1994-95	5.63	17.53	4.51	34.22
1995-96	6.80	20.78	4.99	10.64
1996-97	6.40	-5.88	5.62	12.62
1997-98	7.83	22.34	6.25	11.20
1998-99	8.43	7.66	6.94	15.36
1999.00	9.16	8.65	7.78	12.10

Source: Economic Survey. Orissa. 2000-2001.

The Table shows that the growth of per capita income was remained erratic and in declining trend with negative growth in the year 1996-97. On the whole the growth had shown 91.23 per cent in six year with an average annual growth rate of 15.20 per cent. During the same period the growth of motor vehicles registered the total growth of 131.54 per cent and average annual growth rate of 21.92 per cent, higher than the growth rate of per capita income. This means one per cent of economic growth rate instigated 1.44 per cent of road transport system in Orissa. There is direct positive correlation between the growth of state per capita income and growth of motor vehicles. The Coefficient of Correlation calculated is r = 0.9607 which is a highly positive correlation.

Growth of per capita state income and growth of number of motor vehicles in orissa from the year 1993-94 through 1999-2000 is presented graphically in Fig. 7.4. It clearly shows the trend of growth in similar pattern.

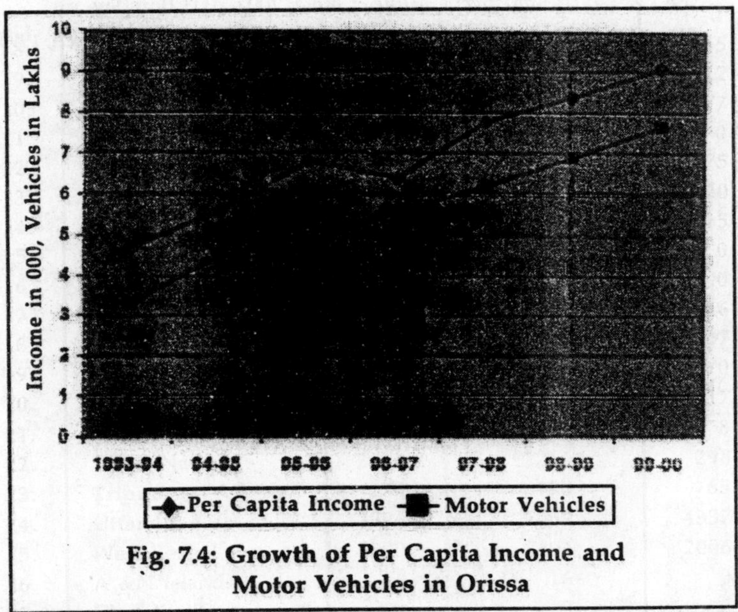

Fig. 7.4: Growth of Per Capita Income and Motor Vehicles in Orissa

Conclusion

Road transport is an important factor for economic development. The economic development is very slow in Orissa. The per capita state income is lowest in the country; Orissa has highest percentage of people below the poverty line. Accordingly, the transport sector has not developed properly. There is high correlation between economic growth and increase in the number of motor vehicles in Orissa which is r= 0.96. The present growth of motor transport in orissa seems to be satisfactory according to the national trend. But more progress is required in this sector to have higher social standard in the state. The growth of road transport would increase only when the economic growth of Orissa would be accelerated.

REFERENCES

1. Dhingra, Iswar C., (1996) *The Indian Economy*. Sultan Chand & Sons. New Delhi.
2. Government of Orissa, (2001) *Economic Survey, 2000-2001*, Bhubaneswar.
3. Owen, Wilfred, (1989)"Transportation and Development" *Journal of Transport Management*, July, 1889.
4. TATA, (2002) *Statistical Outline of India*, 2002-2003 Bombay.
5. World Bank, *India, Transport Sector Long Term Issue*, Report March, 1995.

8

Rural Road

A Key Indicator for Rural Development–Study

Dr. Santosh Kumar Pradhan*
Dr. Rabi Narayana Misra**

Introduction

Rail and road are the body and bones of the surface transportation, whereas rural road is constitute its nerves.

Rural road occupied a key component for rural development, without its place of importance the turning wheel of rural development is locked', it acts as the life line of the rural areas as well as it is the Sine qua-non of nations development. It contributes directly or indirectly to the improvement of living conditions of the rural people. Rural road has promoted agricultural growth, contributing directly to lower transport coats and facilitating the expansion of service sector activities in rural areas. It also helps to reduce regional variations in food prices by facilitating the movement of the food and agricultural commodities.

Rural India which encompasses three-fourth of the country's population living in 5.87 lakh villages which faced problems such as poverty, unemployment, low quality of life, etc. All these un-curable problems of rural India may be rectified by the development of surface transport, it's crucial from the growth of rural economy as well as welfare.

---

* Research Scholar.

Road Network in India

"Road transport is the second important mode of transport in India, total length of road has increased from 4 lakh kilometers in 1950-51 to 33.19 kms. in 2001-02 out of which 15.2 lakh kms, is surfaced and rest 18.0 lakh kms, is un-surfaced. At present India has a total road network covering 2.28 million kilometers which makes the third largest road network in the world.

Act of total roads network of all types in India (24.66 lakh kms.), Panchayat Road constitute 10.54 lakh kms. (42.6) per cent. While P.W.D. roads (940 lakh km.) account for 38.00 per cent, urban roads (2.32 lakh km.) from 9.4 per cent and project roads account for 10.00 per cent. The surfaced roads account for only 56.6 per cent of all types of roads in India. The majority of Panchayat roads remain un-surfaced which constitute about 63 per cent of total Panchayat roads length. The National Highways, State Highways and other PWD road had almost surfaced 83 per cent in India.

Key-Indicator for Rural Development

Availability of fair weather/surfaced roads connecting every village is prerequisite quality of life and economic progress in the rural areas. An efficient rural transportation system especially rural road would accelerate socio-economic development of the countryside in the narrated heads:

(i) Rural road would facilitate quick movement of rural traffic at reduced cost and remove centuries-old social barriers to the mobility of rural folk;

(ii) Rural road would render public administration (revenue and police) more efficient, the benefits of which would ultimately accrue to the rural civilian;

(iii) Rural road help to carry products of horticulture, vegetables, surplus food grains and products of animal husbandry to urban areas;

(iv) Rural road would facilitate the introduction of modern input such as, chemicals, fertilizers and improved seeds and the use of pesticides;

(v) Rural road creates new job opportunities by reducing rural unemployment problems with facilitating migration of labour from rural to urban areas;

(vi) Rural road changes social infrastructure by providing health and education facilities to rural mass;

(vii) Rural road helps sustainable development of Agro-based, cottage industries and raised sources of income for rural artisans;

(viii) Rural Road can mobilized natural resources for manufacture the final products.

Rural Road Scenario of Orissa

It is said that Orissa is a totally backward state in the country about 88 per cent population live in village and depends on agriculture and allied activities from its sustain. Development of agriculture in particular and the economy in general, depends on amelioration of rural poverty for development of rural based small-scale and cottage industries, generation of employment opportunities with development of minimum needable facilities the rural road is Since qua-non for rural development in the State. The development length of rural roads in different periods up to 2002 is also clearly reflected in the following Table—8.1. (*See Table on next page*).

The Table—8.1 reveals that the total length rural-roads in the state is shown that the Gram Panchayat roads length in the highest. On District basis Kalahandi is 9955 kms. highest in length. On the basis of Panchayat Samiti roads Nawrangpur is on top. On village roads the basis of Mayurbhanja is highest in length in the state. Because of backwardness of both of these districts the rural roads given top priority to rural upliftment by construction of rural roads with creating new job opportunity, common minimum programme facilities like health, education, marketing of the agricultural products in the urban area.

Study of Relevant

The present chapter is a study of relevant of the Aska Block of Ganjam District. The compiled data have been collected from the Panchayat Samiti registers about the matter of total length of different types of rural roads construction in different Gram Panchayats based up to January, 2004.

Table 8.1: Rural road scenario of the state 2001-2002 (Length in Kms.)

District	*Classified Village Road*	*Village Road*	*G.P. Road*	*P.S. Road*	*Forest Road*
Angul	159	676	7332	799	423
Balasore	31	1317	1682	787	59
Baragarh	45	1060	6560	476	271
Bhadrak	91	777	1572	878	–
Bolangir	90	1137	5827	173	249
Boudh	41	460	3745	814	214
Cuttack	144	1111	2641	814	192
Deograh	100	215	2891	289	98
Dhenkanal	211	518	5670	620	226
Gajapati	37	442	4253	301	107
Ganjam	200	2138	6717	761	480
Jagatsingapur	188	619	1308	673	3
Jajpur	96	874	2656	798	36
Jharsuguda	105	374	2850	348	20
Kalahandi	282	782	9955	517	308
Kandhamala	133	627	5650	532	358
Kendrapara	29	614	2512	684	20
Keonjhar	94	1118	2436	926	252
Khurdha	129	664	4925	595	231
Koraput	391	387	4973	986	224
Malkanagiri	152	672	2954	357	98
Mayurbhanja	245	2221	6641	1383	1018
Nawarangapur	147	872	5127	1305	12
Nayagarh	99	334	5497	506	307
Nuapada	20	453	4133	504	280
Puri	2	1044	7282	574	16
Rayagada	175	756	4032	751	198
Sambalpur	43	870	6499	603	759
Sonepur	1	385	3032	313	42
Sundargarh	9	1204	8820	801	618
Total	**3570**	**24821**	**139973**	**20372**	**7242**

Source: Districts at a glance-2003 Orissa.

Aska Block is the one of the most important block in Ganjam District. It covers 18472 hectares of geographical area, with 27 Nos. of Gram Panchayats, 134 Nos. of total village out of which 110 Nos. villages are revenue villages and 24 Nos. of Hamlets village. One public Health Centre is situated at Balisira, three numbers of Sub-Centres at Vetanai, Jayapur, Nalabanta, One Veterinary Dispensary at Aska. In Education it consisted of 109 Nos. Primary Schools, 17 Nos. Govt. U.P. (UGME) Schools, 26 Nos. High Schools and 6 Nos. of Colleges. It is the centre Unit of Ganjam District for forecasting with the place of communication, culture and education.

Panchayat Samiti Roads of Aska Block

Aska Block Office is situated at Central place of different Gram Panchayats far away Distance about 10 kilometers, in this manner the rural road is necessary for enter connection of the Block Office for not only maintainable the law and order system of the State Bureaucracy and Legislature but also formation of the Social need how of the rural people with removal all obstacles are created by facts and factors. Different varieties of roads in Gram-Panchayat level is also clearly mentioned on the Table—8.2. (*See on next page*).

Table—8.2 reveals that the inter connection of villages to Gram Panchayats and Block has been observed that the metal and mud-roads are topmost, than the concrete and pichu roads, in different Grama Panchayats. Now the food for works programme formation each and every Panchayats by providing facilitating of proper transportation with sanction of money for construction of concrete road of each village not for develop the infrastructure but for implemented of soil conservation today.

So far as for better transportation good condition of road is necessary but in mainly meanwhile that most of Panchayat is cover with mud road land, it also creates difficulties during the rain season when the heavy rain washed away the soil from the road than the difficulties arised for interconnection with social need how.

Table 8.2: Panchayat Samiti roads of Aska Block

Sl. No.	*Gram Panchayat*	*Varieties of Roads in Mts.*				
		Concrete	*Pichu*	*Metal*	*Mud*	*Total*
1.	Allipur	N.A.	N.A.	N.A.	N.A.	N.A.
2.	Ballichhai	3850	–	2150	7050	13050
3.	Ballisira	10500	–	2000	1750	14250
4.	Babanpur	2850	1000	–	1750	6600
5.	Badakholi	2375	–	5125	2750	10250
6.	Bangarada	N.A.	N.A.	N.A.	N.A.	N.A.
7.	Baragam	N.A.	N.A.	N.A.	N.A.	N.A.
8.	Benapata	N.A.	N.A.	N.A.	N.A.	N.A.
9.	Chadhiapalli	N.A.	N.A.	N.A.	N.A.	N.A.
10.	Debabhumi	1660	1050	8000	4750	15460
11.	Gangapur	N.A.	N.A.	N.A.	N.A.	N.A.
12.	Gunthapada	2850	–	310	3840	7000
13.	Gahangu	N.A.	N.A.	N.A.	N.A.	N.A.
14.	Haridapadar	3950	500	1750	16050	22250
15.	Kalasandhapur	4700	–	–	–	4700
16.	Kamagada	2450	3000	5950	1760	13160
17.	Kendupadar	1800	1000	4200	6000	13000
18.	Kharia	N.A.	N.A.	N.A.	N.A.	N.A.
19.	Mangalpur	N.A.	N.A.	N.A.	N.A.	N.A.
20.	Munigadi	1170	500	1010	750	3430
21.	Jayapur	1250	750	2750	3000	7750
22.	Nalabanta	10001	2000	5007	6900	23908
23.	Nimina	2350	–	5500	6500	14350
24.	Pandiapathar	3775	500	625.	5625	10525
25.	Sidhanai	N.A.	N.A.	N.A.	N.A.	
26.	Khandadeuli	1580	250	2590	1760	6180
27.	Bhetanai	2375	–	3500	5125	10990

Source: Compiled from P.S. Report—2004.

Suggestions

For better standard of living of the rural civilization major suggestions and remedies are given, which, would alleviate to great extent the problem of rural-road:

(i) The cost of laying roads and maintaining them is increasing with every passing year;

(ii) Reduction in drudgery and the load on the animals should receive as much priority as introduction modern mode of transport;

(iii) Keep away to the private sector to build, operate and transfer (B.O.T.) of Rural Road Network;

(iv) Local Panchayats and NGOs have directly involved in motivating peoples participation on the creation of up-keep of community assets of rural-roads;

(v) New rural motor transport scheme may be introduced to solve the problem of rural-road management system;

(vi) Local Panchayat, Zilla Parishad, State, P.W.D. should have funds duly earmark for maintenance at regular interval of rural roads;

(vii) An independent board should be setup for development, maintenance, financing and controlling of rural-road transport.

Conclusion

The rural-road is a key-indicator for rural development. It is the duty and responsibility of every rural citizen to take care, involvement in the designed, construction, operation and maintenance of rural road not better standard of living but for change the rural scenario with formation of Rural Transportation Network present day.

REFERENCES

1. P.K. Dhar, Road Transportation System in Indian Economy, p. 550.
2. Dr. R.L. Hyderabad, Rural Transportation-Problem and Management, *Kurukshetra* October 1996, p. 101.
3. K.L. Raju, Rural Network, *Kurukshetra*, September 2000, p. 41.
4. District at a Glance, Orissa, 2003.

9

Surface Transport for Rural Development

With Special Reference to Rural Roads

Dr. Jagabandhu Samal*

The development of rural infrastructure is crucial for the growth of rural economy and rural welfare particularly development of transport and communication has been considered as sine qua non for economic and social development. The development of rural transport assumes special importance from the point of view of economic integration of rural areas with the administrative, marketing and servicing centres. It breaks isolation of villages by evoking social awakening in rural masses; it can promote political cohesion and strengthen country's defence. It contributes directly or indirectly to the living conditions of the people. Poverty assessment studies made in India emphasise the close relationship between isolation and rural poverty. It is a fact that lack of rural connectivity and lack of mobility pose several constraints to rural development.

Significance of Rural Transport

Rural India encompasses three-fourth of the country's population. Rural people mainly depend upon agriculture and allied activities for their living. The rural economy in India is characterised by low income levels, not even adequate to ensure

* **Rtd. Reader in Economics, Consultant, IGNOU, Sub-Regional Centre, Koraput.**

quality of life compatible with physical well being even after 52 years of planning wherein the development of rural areas and rural people has been the central concern of planned development. It is no wonder that in terms of life expectancy, educational attainment and income, the 1996 Human Development Report of UNDP placed India 135th way below Vietnam and even Myanmar.

In-spite of this the priority accorded to agriculture, irrigation and power etc., under the planned era has definitely brought about a revolution in agriculture. Several lakh hectares of uncultivated land has gradually been brought under irrigation. Agricultural production reached a record level of about 150 million tones by 1991-92. But the success in "green revolution" "white revolution", "yellow revolution" etc. could not bring about equitable distribution of the fruits of these revolutions and stabilise prices. The economic conditions of the farmers remained the same and they could not be liberated from the clutches of middlemen and unscrupulous traders.

Rural transport system facilitate free flow of rural produce to consumer centres and agricultural inputs to rural areas. It also helps proper distribution of available food and ensures better prices to the prodecurs. At the same time, it reduces wastage of perishable goods. It helps the farmers and other rural artisans in supplementing their earning and saves them from squeezing brokers and middlemen. Therefore, without an efficient and effective rural transport system, we cannot expect proper distribution of rural produce and stabilisation of their prices in general and improvement in the economic condition of the farmer in particular.

The Indian Scenario

Ours is an agricultural country with about 6,00,000 villages. The system of transportation in India presents a pathetic picture, be it rural or urban. About rural areas, the less said the better. There are many villages still in our country which have little access and in many cases no access to roads. Though much emphasis was laid down on the improvement of rural roads under various Five Year Plans, they still remained uneven Kutcha roads impassible during the rainy season. Poor communication system restricts markets or mandis hindering cheap or rapid movement of agricultural produce. Hence, rural transportation has a crucial role to play in the economic development of the village in our country.

Rural Road Set-Up

However, the rural transportation scenario prevailing in our country is quite primitive. Animals and animal drawn vehicles are the principal means of transport in remote rural areas. Out of the modes of transport in rural areas, the bullock cart plays an important role. Inspite of its antiquity not less than 70 per cent of the total volume of our internal freight in rural areas is carried by bullock carts. Their number is almost 150 lakh now. It is said that our country is of carts, not of cars, where one person out of 40 owns a cart and one out of 1200 owns a car. Today in India 150 lakh bullock carts carry roughly 170 million tones of goods per year. Camel carts and horse carts are also other modes of transport in some parts of rural India. Motor bus transport was mainly confined to cities and towns very recently. Now it has started penetrating into remote areas. But unfortunately, its rate of growth is not satisfactory, mainly because of the sorry plight of the roads. There are many villages which are not accessible by motor transport even now. It is now observed that with gradual opening of villages by all-weather roads in some areas, mini motor vehicles and auto rickshaws are entering into villages to serve the rural people. Bicycle has been an inseparable part of an average Indian. In addition to carrying persons, carrying of products like milk, vegetables, etc. by bicycle is the guess of anybody. Similarly, tricycle is one of the modern continuances progressively used by traders both in towns and villages to market various products. In hilly tracks and mountains animals like donkeys, horses and even elephants are used in transporting men and materials. Camels are used in deserts as a popular mode of transport. Now, where it is possible trucks and tractor-trailers are used to carry goods from villages to towns and vice versa. Thus, the rural transport irrespective of the mode is very significant for the development of rural economy.

Present Status of Rural Road Connectivity

Several studies have established that connecting the habitations to a neighbouring market or the main road leading to market enhances the incomes of not only primary agricultural producers but all those engaged in rural services and trade. Therefore, achieving full rural accessibility in a time bound manner is an important objective for ensuring rural prosperity.

In the national programme of Minimum Needs Programme (MNP) introduced during the Fifth Plan, the rural programme figured prominently. Its objective was to link all villages with a population of 1500 and above with all weather roads by the end of the Fifth plan. In hilly, tribal and coastal areas, where the population is relatively dispersed, the idea was to go by a cluster of villages of the like size. The Seventh Plan document envisaged linking all villages with a population of 1000 and above by the end of the plan period. Since the population in the hilly tribal, coastal and desert areas is sparse and settlements are located at long distances from one to the other, MNP norm for rural roads was revised during the VII plan. For example, there would be cent per cent linkage to villages with a population of over 500 during the time frame of 10 years and 50 per cent linkage to villages with a population of 200-500 during the same period. For tribal, coastal and desert areas was decided to have cent per cent linkages to villages with a population of over 1000 and 50 per cent linkage to villages with a population of 100-1000 during the 10 years time frame.

The table given below shows the villages connected with roads as on 31st March 1995.

Table 9.1:

Population size of the villages	*Total No. of villages*	*No. of villages connected by roads*	*Percentage of connected villages to total villages*
< 1000	459445	172062	37.45
1000-1500	58027	44031	75.88
1500>	71621	65698	91.73
Total	**589093**	**281791**	**47.83**

Source: Centre for monitoring Indian Economy December, 1999, p. 127.

It would be seen from the table above that out of 5.89 lakh villages in the country only 48 per cent of villages were connected with roads as on 31st March 1995. In other words, 52 per cent of villages did not have road connectivity. It is needless to say that availability of fair weather/surfaced roads connecting every village is a pre-requisite for improving the quality of life and economic progress in rural areas.

Pradhan Mantri Gram Sadak Yojana

Government of India launched the Pradhan Mantri Gram Sadak Yojana (PMGSY) on 25th December 2000. Its objective was to provide road connectivity through all weather roads to all unconnected habitations having a population of more than 1000 persons by the year 2003 and those with a population of more than 500 persons by the end of Tenth Plan Period (2007). If there are no unconnected habitations (of the stipulated population criterion) upgradation (to prescribed standards) of the existing roads can be permitted to be taken up under the programme. It is a planned time-bound programme undertaken by the Government of India to provide basic access to all unconnected habitations with population of 500 and more, numbering about 1.5 lakh. There would still be about an equal number of habitations of lower population levels remaining to be provided with a basic access. In the long run, the scheme aims at providing single connectivity to every unconnected habitation of the district by constructing all-weather roads.

In the hilly and tribal areas, with undulating terrain, there are large number of scattered micro villages with few households and less number of persons where connectivity to all villages with all weather roads is really a difficult and costly task. To cite an example, the position of villages with population in various levels of plateaus in undivided Koraput district of Orissa (the then Koraput district since 1992 has been divided into four districts viz., Koraput, Rayagada, Nawarangapur and Malkangiri). The writer presents below in Table—9.2 villages classified by population size in different geographical divisions based on the attitudes in Koraput (undivided district).

It would be seen from the Table—9.2 that 46 per cent of the villages in undivided Koraput district had a population less than 200 and 76.4 per cent of the villages had a population less than 500 as per 1981 census. It would be again noticed from the table that concentration of micro-villages with population less than 500 was more pronounced in Malkangiri, Koraput and Rayagada plateaus where it varied between 70 and 85 per cent and in 2000 ft. plateau (Jeypore, Nawarangapur Sub-division) it was 53.2 per cent. The dotting of small and isolated villages in the region (old undivided Koraput district) makes the communication difficult and would increase the cost of road construction.

Table 9.2: Villages classified by population size in different geographical divisions based on the altitudes in Koraput (undivided) district in 1981

Sl. No.	*Plateaus/ Sub-divisions*	*No. of habited villages*	*Percentage of villages with size of population*					*% of tribal rural population*
			<200	*200-499*	*500-999*	*1000-1999*	*2000-more*	
01	Koraput Sub-division (excluding Narayanpatna P.S. area) (3000 ft. plateau)	924 (100)	44.1	35.1	14.4	5.2	0.12	57.8
02	Jeypore and Nawarangapur Sub-division (2000 ft. Plateau)	1553 (100)	21.2	31.0	28.8	15.4	3.6	57.2
03	Rayagada & Gunupur Sub-divisions (including N.Patna PS 1000 ft Plateau)	2679 (100)	64.0	20.9	7.3	1.2	0.6	65.3
04	Malkangiri Sub-divisions (500 ft. Plateau)	701 (100)	35.5	35.5	20.1	7.5	1.4	62.4
	Total	**5857 (100)**	**46.1**	**30.3**	**15.6**	**6.4**	**1.6**	**60.2**

Source: a. Census of India, 1981, Series 16, Orissa Part-II-A pp. 182-185.

b. Samal Jagabandhu, Some Aspects of Tribal Economy—A Case Study of Koraput District (1992) -Ph.D. Thesis, p. 95.

The available data on the position and progress of PMGSY in two tribal districts of KBK region (i.e. Koraput and Malkangiri) is given below in Table—9.3.

Table 9.3:

New Connectivity	*1000 +*		*500-999*		*250-499*		*Less than 250*		*Total*	
	Kpt	*Malkn*	*Kpt*	*Malkn*	*Kpt*	*Malkn*	*Kpt*	*Malkn*	*Kpt*	*Malkn*
Total No. of habitants	92	161	160	364	206	700	168	958	628	2181
Total No. of connected habitation	29	103	41	159	52	228	34	271	158	761
Total No. of unconnected habitations	63	58	119	205	154	472	134	685	470	1420
Habitations coverage PMGSY 2000-01	3+ *2	9+ *3	2+ *7	6+ *4					5+ *9	15+ *7
Habitations coverage PMGSY 2001-02	8	10		9					8	19
Habitations coverage PMGSY 2003-04	5	4	3	11		10		4	8	29
Habitations coverage PMGSY 2004-05	13	6	1	8		5		4	14	23
Balance unconnected Habitations	22	28	106	167	154	457	134	677	426	1327

Source: Office of the Rural Work Department, Koraput 2004 (July).

* Upgradation of roads.

From the table it would be revealed that out of a total of 470 unconnected habitations in Koraput district only 42 habitations (8.9 per cent) have been connected with roads under PMGSY (from 2001 to 2004-05 July). Similarly, out of 1420 unconnected habitations in Malkangiri district only 93 villages were connected (6.5 per cent) with roads under the same programme. Hence, 91.1 per cent villages in Koraput district and 93.5 per cent villages in Malkangiri district are yet to be connected by all weather roads under PMGSY programme. As it would be noticed from the table villages having population less than 500 have not been touched by roads under PMGSY in Koraput district till July 2004. Only 3 per cent villages with population 250-499 range and 1.1 per cent villages with population less than 250 in Malkangiri district could be connected with roads. This is the plight of connectivity in hilly and tribal areas of the state with undulated hilly terrain and scattered micro-village. It is also difficult to link all villages with surface roads in coastal and desert areas, where population is sparse and settlements are located at long distances from one another. Still, sincere efforts have to be made to achieve the targets.

Cost Effective Technology

The task of developing an extensive network of all weather roads connecting nearly all the six lakh villages in India is a gigantic one. Due to resource constraint in our country, it is of utmost importance to develop appropriate technologies for rural road construction. It has to be as far as possible, cost effective based on utilisation of local people, materials and machinery. Helps of the Central Road Research Institute (CRRI) may be taken for the purpose as it has developed a few cost effective technologies for rural road construction.

Maintenance of Rural Roads

Once the roads are built, they must be maintained at least to a minimum level of reasonable standard. The funds available for maintenance is only about 20 to 30 per cent of the actual requirements. The cost of building roads and their maintenance is increasing do with every passing year. The Rural Road Organisations have to do more with scarce resources by optimal utilisation of the available funds by increasing their efficiency level.

It was estimated in 1991 that the total loss attributable to poor road conditions is over Rs. 4000 crores per annum. Bad roads lead to higher fuel consumption and low productivity. It would be necessary to provide sufficient funds for maintenance of roads in rural area to avoid continuing deterioration of roads built with scarce plan resources.

User Responsiveness and Peoples Participation

User involvement in the design, construction, operation and maintenance of roads is necessary to improve responsiveness to the needs of the people. The community initiative for rural road network expansion would benefit the projects in several ways. The financial contribution should come from the community. These facilities are more likely to be well operated and maintained when people are involved in technical design planning and management of the project.

Local Panchayats and NGOs have important roles to play in motivating people's participation on the creation and upkeep of community assets like rural link roads. The experience of World Bank supported projects in Africa, Latin America and Asia indicate that the projects with effective participation of the people in project selection and design as opposed to more centralised design making were much more likely to result in good maintenance of infrastructure.

REFERENCES

1. Govt. of India: Planning Commission—Eighth Five Year Plan Document, 1992.
2. Lahiry, S.C.: Rural Road—A Key Component for Rural Development: *Kurukshetra*, December, 1997..
3. UNDP: Human Development Report, 1999, New York.
4. Raju, K.N.: Rural Road Network—Some Issues—*Kurukshetra*—September, 2000.
5. World Bank: Human Development Report—1995—New York.
6. Moitr. B: Rural Roads and Rural Transportation—A New Challenge—*Kurukshetra*—February, 2001.
7. Singh, J.P.: Transportation and Communication in Rural India—Some Facts: *Kurukshetra*, February, 2001.
8. Ramanujam, K.N.: Rural Transport in India *Kurukshetra*, August 1994.
9. Samal J.: Some Aspects of Tribal Economy—A Case Study of Koraput District (Ph.D. Dissertation), Poona University, 1992.

10

Role of Transport in Public Sector Undertakings of Orissa

A Study of O.R.T. Co. Ltd.

Sudhansu Sekhar Nayak*
Dr. Rabi Narayana Misra**

Introduction

Public Sector Undertaking plays a vital role in all socialistic countries in their development plan. They aimed at getting greater, quicker, better and more economical results to build socialism. In modern times, the Government also undertakes business, Railways, Posts and Telegraphs, Radio Broadcasting, Irrigation Projects etc. were owned and managed by the Government even before. After independence the Government nationalized Life Insurance Corporation, Reserve Bank of India, The Imperial Bank of India and fourteen major banks. Thus, the public sector has expanded considerably since independence especially since beginning of the First Plan. When a business undertaking is owned and controlled by the state, it is called a public or state enterprise. We may also say that the business undertaking is in the public sector.

An efficient and cheap system of transport is essential for rapid development of agriculture, industry and trade. It plays an

* **Mr. Nayak, Lecturer in Commerce, Ramanarayan College, Dura–10 (Gm) Orissa.**

** **Dr. Misra, Professor in MBA, SMIT, Ankuspur, Berhampur (Orissa).**

important role in economic development of a country. Without a good and efficient system of transport, it will not be possible for a country like India to achieve desired progress. In other words, transport is a key factor in economic development. It is rightly said that if agriculture and industry are the body and the bones of a national economy, transport and communication are its nerves.

Transport is a means to carry men and materials from one place to another. It involves movement of goods, merchandise and services from where their marginal utility is less to places where their marginal utility is high. Thus, transportation is medium of enhancing the marginal utilities of scarce economic resources to their desirable levels. Hence, it affects the productivity and service sectors of the economy which are ultimately influenced by the customs, habits, traditions and the social organizations.

Scope and Objectives

The present study will act as a comprehensive aid to the existing operational reports of the organization. The defective doubts and shortcomings should be removed and will give a greater contribution for a healthy Government and management. At present we think about the loss of Orissa Road Transport Company Limited (O.R.T. Co. Ltd.) its financial, managerial and labour problems and their removal. The study aims at finding out, what are the factors responsible for loss and what are the remedial measures taken to eradicate loss from the ORT Co. Ltd.

The period of the study has been divided into two phases for the purpose of comprehensive analysis. The first phase related to the period between 1978-79 to 1989-90 and the second phase consists of 1990-91 to onwards because of the two company merged as one corporation known as "Orissa State Road Transport Corporation" (OSRTC) became effective from 16th August 1990.

About the Road Transport

In the surface transport system, both for the movement of passengers and goods, road transport is of crucial importance. There is a wide variety of mechanized and non-mechanized vehicles in the state for road traffic which provides some choice to people to travel and transport goods according to their requirements and paying capacity. In view of its characteristics of easy availability and flexibility of operation, adaptability to individual needs, door-to-door service and reliability, road transport is ideally suitable for short and medium distances, except for bulk movement of goods and mass transit of passengers. Motor transport is also the main mechanized means of transport in hilly and rural areas not served by railways. Further, roads and road transport provide the basic infrastructure for the economic development of backward areas and serve as a feeder service to rail traffic, ports and habours. There are many kinds of vehicles operating on the road. They are thelas, bullock carts, tongas, rickshaws and motor vehicles such as motor cars, jeeps, buses, trucks, motor vans, etc. Table—10.1 presents information on different types of motor vehicles on road in Orissa during the period 1999-2000 to 2003-2004. (*See on next page*)

The Table—10.1 reveals that the number of Motor Vehicles on road of all categories in the state increased from 12,21,070 in the year 2002-03 to 12,71,864 in the year 2003-2004 registering a growth of 13.45 per cent. During the 2001, the number of vehicles in the state per thousand square kms. was 5,622 and per lakh population was 2378 which has increased to 8168 and 3343 respectively during the year 2004. There are 5,297 buses travelling in the state during the year 2003-04. During the year 1991, the number of buses available per lakh population was 09, which increased to 14 during the year 2004. Similarly the number of goods vehicles available per lakh population increased from 84 during the year 1991 to 258 during the year 2004.

Transport Development During Plans in Orissa

The programmes of transport development occupy a significant place in one Five Year Plans. Transport has been seen as the basic infrastructure which is crucial for the success of a development plan. The progress of transport sector under Five Year Plans has been explained in the Table—10.2.

Table 10.1: Motor vehicles on road in Orissa during the period 1999-2000 to 2003-04

Sl. No.	*Types of Vehicles*	*No. of Vehicles as on*					*Percentage increase over 2002-03*
		31.03.00	*31.03.01*	*31.03.02*	*31.03.03*	*31.03.04*	
1.	Goods Vehicle, (Truck, Lorries, Three Wheelers, Tractors & Trailors etc.	60,059	67,743	77,147	84,268	94,859	12.6
2.	Public/Private Bus	4,372	4,499	4,787	4,946	5,297	7.1
3.	Motor Car/Jeep/Taxi	45,660	51,979	58,670	66,691	80,510	20.7
4.	Auto Rickshaw	5,561	6,187	8,787	11,310	15,086	33.4
5.	Motorcycle/Scooter/Moped	6,54,114	7,35,742	8,26,548	9,43,178	10,64,323	12.8
6.	Others (Trakkers)	9,025	9,217	10,616	10,677	11,789	10.4
	Total	**7,78,791**	**8,75,367**	**9,86,555**	**11,21,070**	**12,71,864**	**13.45**

Source: Economic Survey, 2004-05, Planning and Coordination Department, Government of Orissa, Bhubaneswar, p. 12/6.

Table 10.2: Transport development during plan period in Orissa

Sl. No.	Plans		Expenditure	Percentage to Total
1.	First Plan	(1951-56)	271.24	14.7
2.	Second Plan	(1956-61)	603.75	7.0
3.	Third Plan	(1961-66)	3,846.00	17.1
4.	Annual Plans	(1966-69)	1,737.02	13.9
5.	Fourth Plan	(1969-74)	1,663.34	6.7
6.	Fifth Plan	(1974-78)	2,858.64	6.3
7.	Annual Plans	(1978-80)	23.73	6.1
8.	Sixth Plan	(1980-85)	108.25	7.2
9.	Seventh Plan	(1985-90)	232.8	7.17
10.	Annual Plans	(1990-92)	N.A.	N.A.
11.	Eighth Plan	(1992-97)	711.93	10.16
12.	Ninth Plan	(1997-02)	714.02	5.90
13.	Tenth Plan	(2002-05)	522.20	9.78

Source: Economic Survey, 2004-05, Planning and Coordination Department, Bhubaneswar. P– ANX – 1.

N.A.: Not Available.

Table—10.2 shows that during 3rd Plan, the expenditure of transport sector was highest which was Rs. 3846 crore (17.1 per cent) and lowest during 9th Plan which was Rs. 714.02 crore (5.90 per cent) in Orissa out of the total expenditure. During first three year of the Tenth Plan Period (2002-05), the expenditure of transport sector in Orissa was 522.20 lakh (9.78 per cent) out of the total expenditure.

A Brief Profile of ORT Co. Ltd.

The Orissa Road Transport Company Limited (ORT Co. Ltd.) is a tripartite Joint Stock Company with participants of State Government, Union Government through Southern Eastern Railway and shareholders. It was incorporated on 1-12-1950 under the Companies Act VII of 1913 for Nationalization of Road Transport with a view to adequate efficient, economical and property coordinated road transport services to accelerate development in rural and hilly areas where 80 per cent of the people live and also to bring Rail-Road Co-ordination. It is a Government company under Section-617 of the Indian Companies Act as 98.4 per cent of the share capital is contributed by the State and Central Government. It is also a State Government undertaking as defined under Section 68 (A) of the Motor Vehicles Act. It was formed when the passenger transport facilities were very poor in the country. The registered office of the company is at Berhampur (GM). The company commenced its business from 1-1-1951 and during these 55 years of operation of bus services, it has put all efforts for implementing its objectives and inspite of various difficulties hurdles and obstacles it has progressed well.

There being no private competition till 1973-74, the position of the company both economically and in operation was very sound. It earned profit to the extent of Rs. 415.47 lakh and adding depreciation it worked out to Rs. 651.88 lakh during the period from 1951-52 to 1973-74. It contributed to Central Government Exchequer amounting to Rs. 239.84 lakh by way of income-tax, paid dividend to an extent of Rs. 56 lakh to the share holders, owned fixed assets worth Rs. 122.33 lakh, investment of Rs. 34.62 lakh in shape of Government securities and others and working capital of Rs. 59.69 lakh. It could afford employment opportunities to 2,129 people by the end of 1973-74. It was self dependent and has never gone for loan assistance till 1971-72. On account of law equity, the company had gone for the first time for loan assistance for purpose of vehicles for expansion programme during the period from 1971-72 to 1974-75.

Management of the Company

The company was managed by a Board of Directors consisting of four members nominated by the State Government of Orissa, two by the Union Government through the South Eastern Railway and one member elected by the Private shareholders. The Board of Directors held four meetings during the year and considered various matters brought up before them. The day-to-day affairs of the company were managed by the Chairman-Cum-Managing Director who was an I.P.S. Officer of the State.

Operational Territory of the Company

The company operated his services mainly in the district of Ganjam, Phulbani, Puri and part of Cuttack. Besides the services in these areas, services connecting important places like Rourkela, Bolangir, Jeypore, Bhawanipatna, Nawarangpur, Tata (Bihar), Visakhapatnam (Andhra Pradesh), Durgapur (West Bengal) were continued to operate.

For administrative convenience, the operational sphere of the company had been divided into six zones with headquarters at Berhampur, Bhanjanagar, Jatnai, Bhubaneswar, Phulbani and Cuttack. Besides, eight unit offices at the following places also continued to function:

1. Aska
2. Paralakhemundi
3. G. Udyagiri
4. Boudh
5. Odagam
6. Banki
7. Khurda
8. Puri

About OSRTC

Orissa State Road Transport Corporation (OSRTC) a public sector undertaking has been providing transport services and amenities to passengers, travel concession to certain categories of passengers and has been operating/regulating inter-state routes with reciprocal arrangement with other states since its inception in 1974. OSRTC acquired to ORT Co. Ltd. with effect from August 1990. The corporation has been incurring losses over the years owing to reasons like fare structure, need to operate on un-economic routes, over staffing etc. In order to revamp OSRTC and to meet the growing need of the travelling public, Government have decided to make 100 'Off-road' buses of OSRTC Road-worthy after major repairs steps are being taken to purchase 100 new buses for the corporation. A Voluntary Retirement Scheme (VRS) has been introduced to downsize the corporation and a private agency ticketing system has been introduced to enhance the earnings of the corporation.

Analysis

The analysis of the data is made under two heads:

1. Financial Analysis of ORT Co. Ltd., from the Period 1978-79 to 1989-90

The financial analysis of the ORT Co. Ltd., from the period 1978-79 to 1989-90 is explained in Table—10.3.

Table 10.3: Financial analysis of ORT Co. Ltd. from the period 1978-79 to 1989-90

(Rs. in lakh)

Year	*No. of Buses on Road*	*Total Debt*	*Current Assets*	*Current Liabilities*	*Working Capital*	*Net Loss*	*No. of Passengers Carried (in Lakh)*
1978-79	320	152.77	54.20	75.52	(-)21.32	(-)38.84	226.39
1979-80	260	224.52	59.12	106.03	(-) 46.91	(-)53.88	234.06
1980-81	249	379.49	54.16	163.26	(-)109.10	(-)117.78	220.81
1981-82	242	570.36	69.54	241.25	(-)171.71	(-)167.77	216.79
1982-83	247	710.02	85.73	304.94	(-)219.21	(-)221.39	196.24
1983-84	251	1052.06	78.70	430.18	(-)351.48	(-)212.63	210.76
1984-85	235	679.99	127.45	127.38	0.07	(-)226.73	193.16
1985-86	228	1076.94	116.02	198.92	(-) 82.90	(-) 283.72	170.51
1986-87	251	1238.48	106.87	216.46	(-) 109.59	(-)263.61	172.49
1987-88	248	1335.86	122.02	256.65	(-) 134.63	(-)288.33	178.70
1988-89	246	1428.22	131.81	278.39	(-)146.58	(-)288.20	173.20
1989-90	241	1632.19	153.47	291.46	(-)137.99	(-)297.92	171.49

Source: Audited Director's Report and Statement of Accounts of ORT Co. Ltd., from the year 1978-79 to 1989-90.

Table—10.3 shows that the ORT Company started losing from the year 1978-79 onwards. The company miserably failed in generating any profits during this period of study. The minimum net loss amounted to Rs. (-) 38.84 lakh in the year 1978-79 and the maximum net loss amounted to Rs. (-) 297.92 lakh in the year 1989-90. Further the company on an average made a net loss of Rs. (-) 119..93 lakh per annum during this period. The total debt of the company also increasing at a faster rate except the year 1984-85. However, the average debt burden of the company was Rs. 1076.66 lakh per annum. The number of buses of ORT Co. Ltd. on road have decreased over the years. The corporation carried 226.39 lakh passengers in the year 1978-79 which has been decreasing 171.49 lakh in the year 1989-90.

2. Activities of OSRTC from the Period 1992-93 to 2003-04

The Table—10.4 depicts the activities of OSRTC from the year 1992-93 to 2003-04.

Table 10.4: Activities of OSRTC in the State of Orissa

(Rs. in Lakh)

Year	*Fleet Strength*	*No. of Buses of Road*	*Capital Investment*	*Employment (No.)*	*Number of Passengers carried (In Lakh)*
1992-93	915	716	9,319.24	7437	404.44
1993-94	954	725	9,549.24	6628	415.82
1994-95	834	589	11,192.71	6467	348.39
1995-96	836	493	11,587.71	6221	224.86
1996-97	799	395	11,982.71	5906	190.19
1997-98	753	324	12,582.71	5583	148.94
1998-99	755	306	12,942.71	4922	173.85
1999-00	615	272	13,641.03	4485	167.90
2000-01	383	254	13,498.03	3492	186.40
2001-02	297	251	13,498.03	2419	190.55
2002-03	265	241	13,498.08	1602	70.07
2003-04	260	233	13,498.03	1387	58.16

Source: Economic Survey, 2004-05, Government of Orissa, Bhubanswar, p. 12/8.

Table—10.4 shows that, the total fleet strength of the corporation was 260 with 233 buses on road playing in 107 routes of which 20 are inter-state routes during the 2003-04. The corporation carried 58.16 lakh passengers providing employment to 1387 persons during the year. Although the capital investment has increased, the fleet strength and the number of buses on road have decreased over the year. However, it has been sustaining losses over the year. Although, the corporation made a loss of Rs. 552.10 lakh during the 2001-02, it earned a profit of Rs. 65.35 lakh during the period 2003-04.

Suggestions

Following are some suggestions for proper utilization of funds of ORT Co. Ltd. for improve its financial condition:

1. It is suggested that due to shortage of funds of the ORT Co. Ltd., no new buses are to be purchased, and it mostly depend on loan;
2. The management has not able to do timely fare revision, keeping in view of the rate of price hike, due to increase of petrol, diesel and other products;
3. Due to critical financial position on account of continued losses faced by the ORT Co. Ltd., the replacement of the buses could not be made possible in time. So, superannuated vehicles decreased in the fleet and maintenance cost also decreased abnormally;
4. The ORT Co. Ltd., has gone for borrowing for replacement of asset, the loan burden has become very heavy. On account of such financial stringency, it is suggested that the company could liquidate the loan instalments and interest thereon in time;
5. It is suggested that the ORT Co. Ltd., has not continued uneconomical routes operated in rural and hilly areas on social obligations as public utility services.

REFERENCES

1. Dhingra, I.C., Indian Economy, *Sultan Chand and Sons,* New Delhi, 2004.
2. Tandon, B.C., Management of Public Enterprises. *Chaitanya Publishing House,* Allahabad, 1978.

3. Acharya, B.B. and Ghosh, S. Transport, *Kalyani Publishers*, New Delhi-1991.

4. Khan, R.R., Transport Management, *Himalaya Publishing House*, Bombay, 1980.

5. Srivastava, S.K., Economic of Transport, *S. Chand and Co. Ltd.*, New Delhi—1981.

6. Jain, J.K., Transport Economics, *Chaitanya Publishing House*, Allahabad, 1987.

7. Kuchhal, S.C. The Industrial Economy of India, *Chaitanya Publishing House*, Allahabad—1987.

8. Dhar, P.K. Indian Economy, *Kalyani Publishers*, New Delhi, 2005.

9. *Annual Reports of O.R.T. Co. Ltd.* from 1978-79 to 1989-90.

10. *Director's Report and Statement of Accounts of ORT Co. Ltd.*, from 1978-79 to 1989-90.

11. *Economic Survey*, Government of Orissa, Bhubaneswar, 2003-04 and 2004-05.

12. *Statistical Abstracts of Orissa*, Bhubaneswar, 2005.

11

Railway Transportation in Orissa

A Study

Prafulla Chandra Mohanty*

Introduction

Indian Railways are owned by the Government of India and the network is scattered throughout the country for transporting goods and passengers at the cheapest possible price. The State Government has nothing to do with the railways directly except making some suggestions and demands. The railways constitute the basic infrastructure for economic growth and its adequacy is therefore vital.

With the innovation of Jameshwatt's stream engine the first railway in India as also in Asia was introduced by the Great India Peninsular Railway Company of England on 16th April 1853. The first train steamed to Thana from Bombay on the 33 km. route. Then gradually the British connected 3 major ports, presidential towns and other strategic places with the capital of India to perpetuate their hegemony and for exploitation of industrial resources for the benefit of Great Britain.

After a long gap of 37 years, i.e. in the year 1890 Orissa got for the first time the opportunity of railway lines during the process of connecting Calcutta and Bombay. The other trunk line from Calcutta to Madras was constructed after five years which gave the next opportunity of expanding the railways through Orissa. For a long time Orissa was not considered as either strategically or economically important. It was only after independence that the railway system as an infrastructural facility for both national and regional development was recognised by the Government.

Analysis of the Study

Table 11.1: Construction of different rail routes in and through Orissa

Sl. No.	*Rail Routes*	*Distance in Kms. (APP)*	*Yr. & Dt. of construction*
(1)	*(2)*	*(3)*	*(4)*
1.	Jharsugda—Rayagada Route ...	63	20-4-1890
2.	Jharsuguda—Goelker ...	169	1-2-1891
3.	Jharsuguda—Sambalpur ...	46	1-2-1893
4.	Kharagpur—Balasore ...	116	17-12-1898
5.	Balasore—Cuttack ...	117	10-01-1899
6.	Cuttack—Bhubaneswar ...	28	01-02-1897
7.	Bhubaneswar Khurda Road ...	21	20-07-1896
8.	Khurda Road—Rambha ...	99	01-03-1896
9.	Rambha—Berhampur ...	48	01-09-1895
10.	Berhampur—Palasa ...	74	01-04-1895
11.	Palasa—Nuapada ...	25	17-12-1895
12.	Nuapada—Vijayanagaram ...	117	20-09-1894
13.	Vijayanagram—Waltair ...	60	15-07-1893
14.	Khurda Road—Puri ...	44	01-02-1897
15.	Tata—Gorumahisani ...	66	1911
16.	Gorumahisani—Badam Pahar ...	24	1922
17.	Rourkela—Koel (River) ...	8	21-01-1922
18.	Koel—Birmitrapur ...	20	17-09-1926
19.	Rajkharsuan—Danguaposhi ...	73	Jan. 1924
20.	Danguaposhi—Gua (Bihar) ...	32	20-02-1925
21.	Gua-Barbil ...	2	16-02-1926
22.	Barbil—Bolanikhadan ...	29	19-04-1960
23.	Nayamandi—Banspani ...	30	18-04-1958
24.	Barbil—Balani (Keonjhar) ...	8	19-04-1960
25.	Sambalpur—Titilagarh ...	182	1960
26.	Kotavalsa—Kirndul (M.P.) ...	436	1960

(Contd...)

(1)	(2)		(3)	(4)
27.	Bondhamunda—Barsuan	...	73	1959
28.	Cuttack—Paradeep	...	85	February 1973
29.	Jhakhapura—Daitari	...	32	1973
30.	Rayagade—Koraput	...	20 (Out of 164 Kms.)	1985
31.	Chatrapur—Indian Rare Earth, Ltd.	...	7	1985

Source: (1) Daily 'Samaja' the 13th April 1981, p. 7.

(2) Daily 'Samaja' the 26th February 1985, p. 4.

From the Table—11.1, it is clear that the growth of railways in Orissa was achieved till today in four phases. The first phase can be termed as the foundation phase which was started from 1890 to 1990. This is the main decade of railway expansion in Orissa. Two main trunk lines were constructed linking Calcutta with Bombay and Madras. These works were carried on the food for work programmes to save the people of Orissa from the then acute famine. The second phase of construction started after twenty years for the second decade, i.e., from 1920-30. The motive behind this construction was to extract and export the mineral wealth of Orissa from Badam Pahar, Gorumahishani and from similar other areas. After this, again the expansion of railways for Orissa remained static for about 25 years. To use the rest of mineral places of Banspani, Barbil, Bolanikhadan more railway lines were joined with the trunk line in the 1950 to decide. In this period Sambalpur was joined with Titilagarh and another line was linked through Koraput from Kota-Valasa to Kirndul to reduce the distance of Vizag port. At the end, the 1970-80 the last decade of railway extension, in the period of which Paradeep and Dietary was connected with the Madras-Howarh trunk line. With a view to supply iron ore, coal to steel plants and to export the mineral treasure of the State through Paradeep and Vizag ports.

From the administration point of view Indian railways are divided into nine zones. Our railways inside whole of Orissa remains under the South-Eastern Railway Zone, the Head Office which is situated at Gardenreach, Calcutta. The said railway zone has seven divisions. Of this our railways inside Orissa comes under the jurisdiction of five such divisions namely, Khurda Road, Kharagpur, Chakradharpur, Bilaspur and Waltair. The Table—11.2 indicates that these divisions create links for Orissa with Andhra Pradesh, West Bengal, Bihar and Madhya Pradesh. Nearly two seventh of the total rail routes of S.E. Railway zones remain inside Orissa which earns more than one third of the profit. Inside Orissa the Khurda Road Division carries the highest route length among other divisions. More of less the route kms. of Orissa in Chakradharpur and Waltair Division is also nearly equal. Bilaspur Division has occupies only 56 route kms. with seven stations in Orissa. With a total 1981 route kms. of railway lines inside Orissa and 240 railway stations and passenger halts as against the 61,000 route kms. of railway lines and 7,100 stations of the nation. Orissa requires more number of stations and passenger halts in order to cope with the national average figure.

Table 11.2: Division-wise rail routes and stations inside Orissa

No. of divisions	*Name of the division*	*State linked*	*Routes Kms. in Orissa (APP.)*	*No. of Railway Station (APP.)*	*% to total route in Orissa*
1.	Khurda road railway division...	A.P., Orissa, W.B...	600	90	32
2.	Waltair railway division...	A.P., Orissa, M.P...	560	55	28
3.	Bilaspur, railway division...	Orissa, M.P...	56	7	2
4.	Chakradharpur railway division...	Orissa, Bihar...	555	60	27
5.	Kharagpur railway division...	W.B., Orissa...	210	30	11
	Total		**1,981**	**242**	**100**

Source: S.E. Railway time table 1976 and 1982 October with Map.

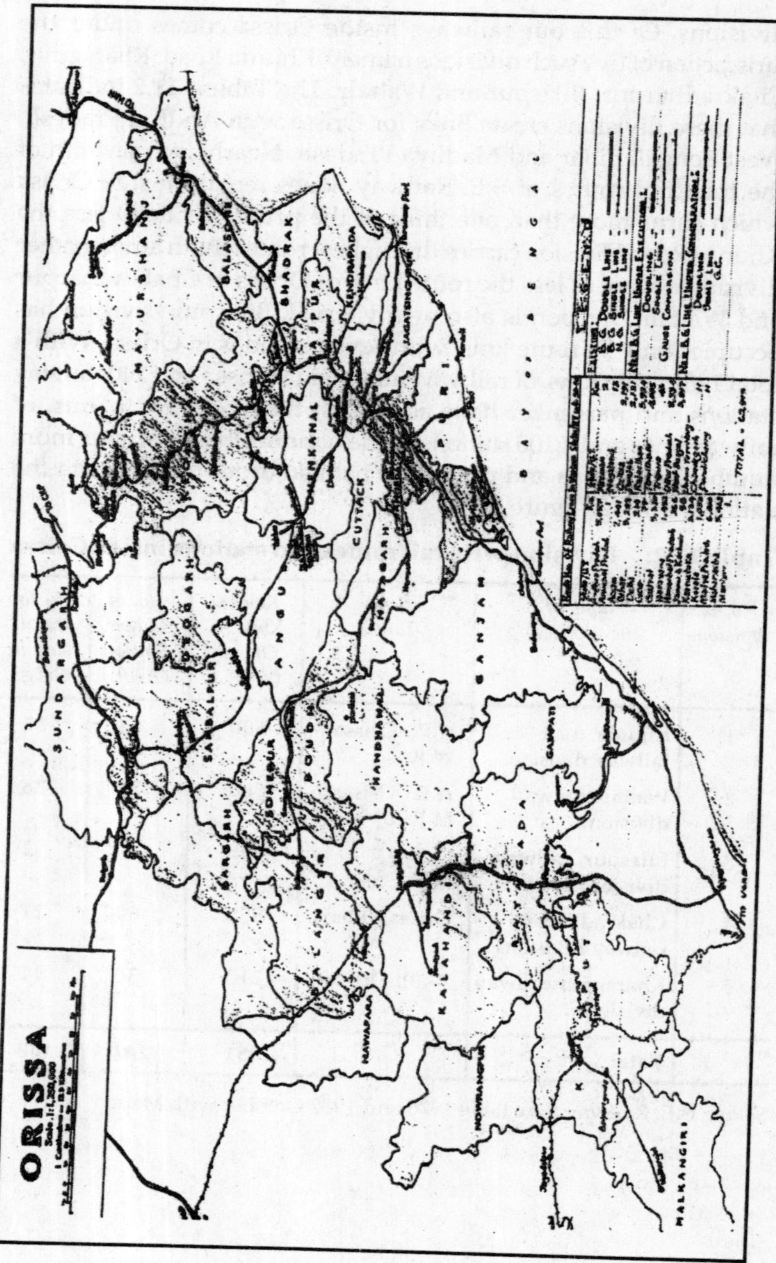
ORISSA
SUNDARGARH
SAMBALPUR
DEOGARH
MAYURBHANJ
BALASORE
BHADRAK
KENDRAPADA
DHENKANAL
ANGUL
CUTTACK
PURI
NAYAGARH
GANJAM
GAJAPATI
BARGARH
SONEPUR
BOUDH
KALAHANDI
NAWAPARA
NOWRANGPUR
MALKANGIRI
BAY OF BENGAL
LEGEND

Table 11.3: Growth of railways (route length in kms.) a comparison

(in Kms.)

	1920-51	*1979-80*	*Increase*	*% of Growth*
Indian Railway ...	53,596	60,933	7,007	13
S.E. Railway ...	5,452	7,007	1,555	27
Railways in Orissa ...	1,300	1,981	681	52

Source: Indian Railways—Journals, Silver Jubilee No. (1956-81).

The findings of Table—11.3, indicates that till 1950-51, Orissa had only one fortieth part of Indian Railways which is very much negligible. But after independence some new lines were constructed and thus in 1979-80 it improved to the one thirteenth part of the national rail routes. It is also evident that prior to independence, Orissa had a share of 1,300 kms. of railways but after independence nearly 700 kms. of new railway lines were constructed by the incessart efforts of the Government.

It is also observed from the Table that there was 13 per cent growth in the Indian Railways, and 27 per cent growth for S.E. Railway during the thirty years. For Orissa, the growth is significant having a figure of more than 50 per cent compared to the base 1950-51 year statistics. But this increase adds only 1 per cent to the growth rate of Indian Railways. To industries the most neglected but potential State like Orissa, some urgent steps should be taken to install more rail links.

The route length of the Indian railways is divided into three different types of railways such as Broad Gauge (B.G.), Metro Gauge (M.G.) and Narrow Gauge (N.G.).

Table—11.4 (*See on next page*) reveals that Orissa acquires 91 per cent of B.G. rail routes and the rest 9 per cent is of N.G. 10 per cent of the total route length is electrified and more the 50 per cent of the B.G. line of the State has no doubles line facility which kills much time and sequence of transportation. To ascertain in the position of the State in the Indian Railway Map, a comparative statement is tabulated in Table—11.5 (five) (*See on page No. 99*) taking into account of the area and population of each state. From the study, it is known that Orissa having 1.25 per cent to her area and

7.4 route kms. per 1 Lakh population as against the national average of 2 per cent and 9 route kms. respectively which remains also less compared to our neighbouring states like Andhra Pradesh, Bihar, West Bengal and Madhya Pradesh. In comparison to area it remains below 12 States and to population below 14 States. So, it is a valid claim of Orissa that she should get more railway lines at least to equalise with the other states of the same mother India.

Table 11.4: Gauge-wise distribution of total route length inside Orissa

Name of the Gauge/ route breadth	*Length in (route) Kms. (nearly)*	*All India % to total route Km.*	*Orissa % to her total routes*
1. Broad Gauge ... 1.676 Metre	1,801	51%	91%
Double line ...	500	...	28 of total B.G.
Electrified ... Double line	200	...	11 of total B.G.
Single line ...	1,101	...	61 of total B.G.
2. Metre Gauge ... 1 Metre	...	42%	0
3. Narrow Gauge ... 0.762 Metre 0.61 metre	180	7%	9
Total ...	1,981	100%	100%

Source: 1. S.E.R. Time Table October, 1982.

2. Annual Report of S.E.R. 1978-79.

The Present Position

After sixty years of independence, Orissa has not received her due share in railways. It is seen that our neighbouring states like West Bengal now has 43 kms. of rail lines per 1000 square kms. of land area, Bihar has 30 kms. Gujarat has 27 kms. and the National average, it is above 19 kms. But it is a matter of great regret that till today being the poorest State of India, Orissa got only 14 kms. of railways per 1000 kms. of her landed area in comparison. Orissa, out of her 30 districts, railway has not touched yet to seven districts like Boudh, Kandhamal, Deogarh, Nayagarh, Kendrapara, Malkangiri and Nawarangpur, the most backward tribal areas of the State.

Table 11.5: State-wise distribution of railway route length in kms.

State	*Railway route Kms. (1978-79)*	*Area in Sq. Kms.*	*Percentage Sq. Kms.*	*Population (As per 1981)*	*Per lakh population*
(1)	*(2)*	*(3)*	*(4)*	*(5)*	*(6)*
Orissa ...	1,948	155,842	1.25	26,272,054	7.4
Andhra Pradesh ...	4,709	276,754	1.7	53,403,619	9.0
Assam ...	2,194	78,523	2.8	19,902,826	11.0
Bihar ...	5,312	173,876	3	69,823,154	7.6
Gujarat ...	5,671	195,984	3	3,396,095	17
Haryana ...	1,456	44,222	3.3	12,850,902	11
Himachal Pradesh ...	256	55,673	0.46	4,237,569	6
Jammu & Kashmir ...	77	222,236	0.035	5,981,600	1.3
Karnataka ...	3,013	191,773	1.5	37,043,451	8
Kerala ...	916	38,864	2.4	25,403,217	3.6
Madhya Pradesh ...	5,739	442,841	1.3	52,131,717	11
Maharashtra ...	5,234	307,726	1.7	62,693,898	8.34
Nagaland ...	9	16,572	0.06	773,281	1.2

(Contd...)

(Table 11.5 Contd...)

(1)	(2)	(3)	(4)	(5)	(6)
Punjab ...	2,139	50,376	4.25	16,669,755	12.8
Rajasthan ...	5,614	342,214	1.63	34,102,912	16.8
Tamil Nadu ...	3,822	130,609	2.9	48,297,456	7.9
Tripura ...	12	10,491	0.1	2,060,189	0.6
Uttar Pradesh ...	8,811	294,413	2.65	110,858,019	7.94
West Bengal ...	3,722	87,853	4.2	54,485,560	6.8
Union Territories—					
Chandigarh ...	11	114	9.6	450.061	2.4
Delhi ...	168	1,485	11.3	6,196,414	2.7
Goa-Daman-Dieu ...	79	3,813	2.1	1,082,117	7.2
Pondichery ...	27	480	6.4	604,136	4.4
Total ...	**60,933**	**328,043**	...	**683810,051**	...

Source: Monorama Year Book, 1982, p. 634.

After a long and consistent demand, in order to avoid the shifting of S.E. Railway Head Office to Orissa, the Central Government has created a new zone named East Coast Railway Zone in 1996 mostly for Orissa which has also not given due importance. The new railway projects which were started in the nineties for Orissa were not given due care and matching budgetary sanction in order to complete within the stipulated time. This makes delay in project completion to highest estimation due to inflation etc.

Table 11.6: Inflated cost of the project

(Rs. in Crores)

Sl. No.	*New Project*	*Distance*	*Year of sanction*	*Original project cost*	*Inflated/ project cost due to delay*
1.	Daitari to Banspani	155 Kms.	1992-93	243	590
2.	Haridaspur to Paradeep	82 Kms.	1996-97	280	350
3.	Khurda to Bolangir (will reduce 245 kms. distance to Mumbai)	289 Kms.	1994-95	360	700

Source: The Oriya Daily "SAMBAD", 17.03.2006, p. 6.

The projects which were sanctioned for Orissa, have not given due care for completion and so the original project castes were inflatted to more than double and so the project completion became the dream for people of Orissa. The Khurda, Bolangir railway line which was approved since 1994-95 with a cost of Rs. 360 crores but till no much progress has made; and so the original project construction cost is going on inflatted to more than Rs. 700 crores. This line after completion will reduce 245 kms. of distance to Mumbai from Bhubaneswar and also to other destinations and this will benefit mostly the backward and no railway line districts of Orissa and other states. From the following Table—11.7 some of the rail projects though approved since long but the budgetary sanction is so miserable, that Orissa people can't have a hope to see the projects completed and useful in any way to them.

Table 11.7: Railway projects of Orissa and the rate of budgetary sanction

Sl. No.	Projects	Distance	Year started	Budgetary sanction (Rs. in Crores)			
				03-04	04-05	05-06	06-07
1.	Dietary-Banspani	155 Kms.	1992-93	79	83	128.61	156
2.	Haridaspur-Paradeep	82 Kms.	1996-97	20	6	20	44
3.	Koraput-Rayagada	164 Kms.	1996-97	1	5	05	2
4.	Kanjigada-Junagada	56 Kms.	1996-97	5	8	8	19
5.	Khurda-Bolangir	289 Kms.	1994-95	15	15	10	20
6.	Angul-Sakirda	98 Kms.	1996-97	2	2	0.10	10
7.	Talcher-Bimalagada	—	1996-97	1	5	5	10

Source: (1) The daily Oriya Sambad, dtd. 17.03.2006, p. 6.
(2) The daily Oriya Sambad, dtd. 20.10.2006, p. 4.

Orissa being the one of poorest states, its development depends upon the different infrastructure system like Rail, Road, Telecommunication etc. Accordingly Orissa has a priority to get his due share like her neighbours atleast on a priority basis. But it is shown from the below Table—11.8 that Central Govt. is not in a mood to give Orissa's minimum rightful demand, the question of sanctioning more rail links in a priority basis does not arise.

Table 11.8: Funds demand by the State Govt. and supplied by Centre

(Rs. in Crores)

Year	*Funds demanded by State Govt.*	*Funds supplied by Centre*	*Difference not made up*
2001-02	505 Crores	178.66	326.34
2002-03	590 Crores	194.00	496.00
2003-04	510 Crores	306.09	204.00
2004-05	650 Crores	366.34	283.70
2005-06	780 Cores	360.00	420.00
2006-07	800 Crores	653.00	147.00
Six yr. Total:	3935 Crores	2058.09	1877.04
Average:	656	243.00	313.00

Source: SAMBAD, The Oriya Daily, dtd. 17.03.2006, p. 6.

It seems that the Railway Ministers sanction funds not on the need basis but mostly on the political basis. This hurts Orissa's railway development.

Berhampur-Gopalpur-Phulbani (175 kms.) Rail link was surveyed for the first time by Britishers and then for several times in nineties and again in 2001. But it was only in the files since long. New it is high time to link Gopalpur Port, Via Phulbani to Bolangir and than to Raipur. The highly neglected backward districts of Orissa—the Malkangiri required to be well connected by rail. These links will add values for Indian Railways from passenger and goods freight. This will not only enhance the income of the railway but also develop the socio-economic conditions of the tribal people by exporting their forestry, mineral, Agricultural and other products of the area and not the least, the total landed area/people which is not neglected and deserted like can be brought to the limelight of the modern civilization.

Conclusion

From the above analysis it is observed that the growth of railways inside a resourceful State like Orissa does not appear to have been specifically designed to meet the growing industrial needs of the State. The benefit if any accruing to Orissa is rather incidental. Till today Orissa did not have its due share in railways as compared with other States. Except the Coastal and Boarder districts of Orissa, the interior part of the state remains completely untouched. Phulbani is till a district which carries no rail routes or lines at all. So steps should be taken to construct new railway links such as Khurda Road to Bolangir, Gopalpur to Berhampur to Aska to Balliguda to Titlagarh, Kesinga to Bhawanipatna to Nawarangpur to Malkangiri, etc. in order to cover an wide backward area of the state.

REFERENCES

1. *Indian Railways Journals* from 1976-82, July, Government of India.
2. The '*Samaja*' of 16th March 1982, 13th March 1981, 26th February 1985, 16th April 1986 and 17th April 1986.
3. *Population Statistics of India*, Government of India.
4. *Orissa Review* p. 13 of January 1982, Public Relation Department, Government of Orissa.
5. *S.E. Railway Time Tables with Maps* from 1976-October, 1982.

6. *Indian Railway Map*, Government of India.
7. *Indian Railways Journal*, Silver Jubilee, November (1956-81), Government of India.
8. *The Orissa Journal of Commerce*, Vol. I, 1987, The Orissa Commerce Association.
9. The '*Samaja*' of 8th February, 2006, The Oriya Daily from BBSR.
10. The '*Samaja*' of 26th October, 2005, The Oriya Daily from BBSR.
11. The '*Sambad*' of 27th February, 2006, The Oriya Daily from BBSR.
12. 'Reference of Orissa', An Indian State of Eastern Region. *Enterprising Publishers*, BBSR, Ed. 1999.
13. *Orissa Review*, pp. 19-24, Information and Public Relation Department, Government of Orissa, April, 1987.
14. *Railway Time Table with Map*, 2006.

12

Road Transport System in Orissa

A Management Look

Dr. Sudhansu Sekhar Nayak*
Dr. Anil Kumar Sahu**
Dr. Rabi Narayana Misra***

Introduction

An efficient and vibrant Road Transport system in a State is the most essential ingredient for the long-term socio-economic and cultural prosperities. It has direct bearing on the quality of the life of the people. With enormous implications embodied, the efficacies of road transport system is inextricably linked with the types and extent of regulatory, management and administrative set up in the State.

The first Indian Motor Vehicle Act was passed in 1914 with only 18 Sections. It conferred powers to local Governments to regulate the use of motor vehicles by way of registrations, licensing and punishments. But with the break of First World War in 1914 and great depression at global level till 1930, the Act almost remained ineffective all over the country. In 1939, the Motor Vehicle Act was enacted with the recommendations of Indian Railway Enquiry

* **Dr. Nayak, Lecturer in Commerce, Ramanarayan College, Dure–10 (Gm) Orissa.**

** **Dr. Sahu, Reader in MBA, Berhampur University, Bhanja Bihar (Orissa).**

*** **Dr. Misra, Professor in MBA, SMIT, Ankuspur, Berhampur (Orissa).**

Committee headed by Wadgewood. The Motor Vehicle Act, 1939 laid the foundation of formal administrative machinery in road transport which functions till date. The Act, besides enforcing restrictions on the movements of vehicles on road in terms of registrations, licensing, permits and penalties in elaborate procedures and rules, ensured the creation of State and Regional Transport Authorities at State and district level all over the country for the first time, of course, in complete collaboration with Police Department. Since then, the administrative structure of the road transport in the State have been reshaped, streamlined and more recognized from time to time with the subsequent enactment of Motor Vehicle Acts and their amendments. The basic rationale behind the need for a strong administration in road transport sector in the State were as follows:

1. Transport is a concurrent subject;
2. The national investment in road transport sector is as high as in other modes of transport and communication like railways, airways, waterways etc.;
3. The road transport department was grossly under staffed;
4. The accelerated pace of road transport cannot be denied in the process of rapid economic development. This essentially requires and efficient management and administration of this vital sector.

With about 15 lakh registered vehicles and annual generation of Rs. 260 crore revenue for the State exchequer, the administrative machinery of the road transport department of the State of Orissa functions in a multidisciplinary approach. Its administration is manned by combined network of civil servants, automobile engineers, police personnel, statisticians and judicial experts.

Scope and Objectives

The main objectives of transport administration are:

- To main and improve the skill management for the department personnel;
- To ensure transparency in the day-to-day management and administration of the officials;
- To enhance the scope of additional resource mobilization in road transport sector;

- To provide a road user friendly transport administration in the State;
- To protect the public interest by making their mobility safe and comfortable on road;
- To expedite the process of modernization for a more efficient, vibrant and productive road transport management system in the state.

Road Network of Central Government

India has 3.3 million kilometers of road network, which is the second largest in the world. Roads occupy an eminent position in transportation as they, as per the present estimate, carry nearly 65 per cent of freight and 87 per cent of passenger traffic. Traffic on roads is growing at a rate of 7 to 10 per cent per annum while the vehicle population growth, for the past few years, is of the order of 12 per cent per annum.

The different categories of roads and authorities responsible for them are:

1. *National Highway*— Central Government (through Ministry of Road Transport and Highways).
2. *State Highways and Major District Highways*— State Governments (PWDs)
3. *Rural Roads and Urban Roads*— Rural Engineering Organizations, Local Authorities like Panchayats and Municipalities.

Ministry of Road Transport and Highways is directly responsible for development of National Highways which aggregate 57737 kms. which, although is only 1.7 per cent of total length, carries about 45 per cent of the road traffic. The National Highways is thus the length, carries about 45 per cent of the road traffic. The National Highways is thus lifeline of the country, connecting the farthest corners and the remotest border areas.

The emphasis is now on development the quality of National Highways, besides expanding the network. The Ministry of Road Transport and Highways has therefore taken up a number of projects and programmes to achieve this goal.

To upgrade the technology and to evolve cost-effective new techniques for design, construction and maintenance of roads and bridges and operation of traffic, this ministry has also taken up a number of studies and research programmes in association with the various Research Institutes and Universities.

The National Highways Development Project (NHDP) has been initiated to upgrade the existing highways to connect the four metropolitan cities Delhi, Mumbai, Chennai and Kolkata by the Golden Quadrilateral and the North-South and East-West Corridors connecting Kanyakumari with Srinagar and Porbandar with Silchar. This project will involve upgradation to four/six laning of about 13,000 kms. of National Highways and is to cost Rs. 54,000 crore. Target years for completion of Golden Quadrilateral and the National Highway Development Project have been set to be 2003 and 2007 respectively. National Highways Authority of India, and organization under the Ministry of Road Transport and Highways has been assigned this task. This is the most ambitious road-building programme and one of the monumental construction projects in the history of modern India and it will be a great challenge for the Ministry of Road Transport and Highways and its organizations to achieve this stupendous task in the short time frame.

In addition, a short-term programme for improving the riding quality of other National Highways has also been initiated. The improvement in Riding Quality Programme (IRQP) aims to cover the entire national highways network in next 5 years.

The State Governments concerned, though which the National Highways are passing, are executing the works on behalf of the Central Government. Preparation of 5-year Plans and Annual Plans and guiding the State PWDs for project preparation, approving the works and monitoring the execution of works are the responsibilities of the Central Government.

The Central Government is also responsible for keeping the entire National Highway Network in traffic worthy condition. As the nodal Ministry in the roads sector, the Ministry of Road Transport and Highways has been taking an initiative to formulate maintenance norms for all categories of roads, including National

Highways. Funds for maintenance of National Highways are being allocated to the extent possible considering the difficult resource position.

This year the Central Government has declared 5694 kms. of roads as National Highways. This has brought the total of National Highways declared in Ninth Plan Period (1997 onwards) to 23,439 kms. Most of these National Highways are in remote, hilly or backward areas and they now require attention to be brought upto National Highways standards.

The resource requirement for removal of deficiencies on National Highways is estimated to at whooping Rs. 1650 Billions. Mobilizing such funds is a big challenge. This is being done by traditional budgetary allocation, as well as, innovative measures like revamping of Central Roads Fund, funding from multi lateral agencies, private sector participation, market borrowing etc.

To meet the challenges of accelerated funding requirements for all categories of roads in the country, the Central Road Fund has been augmented by increasing the levy of cess on petrol to Re. 1/- per litre of petrol and charging a cess of Re. 1/- per litre of diesel. The Central Road Fund Act, 2000 has also been notified on 27-12-2000 to give statutory status.

The Central Road Fund seeks to distribute the total of 100 per cent of cess on petrol and 50 per cent of cess on diesel in the following way:

(i) 57.5 per cent for National Highways;

(ii) 30 per cent for State Roads;

(iii) 12.5 per cent for safety works on Rail-Road crossings.

The ministry of Road Transport and Highways is responsible for administering the share of National Highways and State Roads.

The remaining 50 per cent of the cess on diesel is to be used to develop rural roads. From the generated fund, an intensive programme for the development of rural roads has been taken up. The Ministry of Rural Development, Government of India, is responsible for this programme.

The Ministry is also approving the schemes for improvement of State Roads under Economic and Interstate Importance (E & I schemes). From the revamped Central Road Fund, 10 per cent of the State share will be allocated for E & I Schemes. The sum available for E & I Schemes will be around Rs. 100 crore per annum. The Ministry is formulating guidelines for such schemes and is in the process of calling for estimates of projects from the State Governments for sanction of these E & I Schemes.

In addition, Ministry also provides funds to State Governments and Border Road Development Board for some strategic roads and certain selected roads in far flung and inaccessible areas.

The Ministry of Road Transport and Highways is the nodal Ministry in the country in the roads sector and is the nodal Ministry in the country in the roads sector and is guiding different states for construction and maintenance of quality roads by issuing technical circulars related to different aspects of Highway Engineering and Practice. The Ministry of Road Transport and Highways has prepared specification for Road and Bridge Works, standard drawing for various types of bridges, culverts and junctions. The Indian Roads Congress (IRC), a premiere body of highway engineers in India, is formulating codes and standards for design, construction and maintenance of roads and bridges and for traffic operations.

The Central Government through the Ministry of Road Transport and Highways is also actively involved with International Organizations like World Bank, Asian Development Bank, Japan Bank for International Co-operation for upgradation of the technology and decision making process. This requires continues interaction with organization like ESCAT, BIMSTEC etc. The Ministry of Road Transport and Highway has also signed Memorandum and Understanding with its counterparts in Malaysia and France for co-operation in the areas of Highway Engineering. In many cases, the Ministry of Road Transport and Highways is the nodal Ministry for India in the field of co-operation in Transport sector as a whole.

Analysis

Total road length in the state is 2,38,006 kms. as on 31.03.2004. The different categories of roads explained in Table—12.1.

Table 12.1: Total road length of Orissa

Types of Roads	*Length (in Kms.)*
National Highways	3,193 Kms.
State Expressways	30 Kms.
State Highways	5,102 Kms.
Major District Roads	3,189 Kms.
Other District Roads	6,112 Kms.
Rural Roads	28,365 Kms.
Panchayat Samiti Roads	20,324 Kms.
Gram Panchayat Roads	1,39,942 Kms.
Forest Roads	7,242 Kms.
Urban Roads	18,132 Kms.
Irrigation Roads	6,277 Kms.
GRIDCO Roads	88 Kms.

Source: Economic Survey, 2004-05.

Table—12.1 shows that there are 12 numbers of National Highways as on 31.03.2004 in Orissa. Proposed Coast line road of about 574 kms. from Gopalpur in Ganjam district to Digha. Orissa State Road Transport Corporation (OSRTC) while providing transport service amenities to passengers, also regulates the inter State bus routes with neighbouring States Bengal, Andhra Pradesh and Madhya Pradesh. As on 31.03.2004, the State namely Boudh, Deogarh, Kandhamal, Kendrapara, Malkangiri and Nayagarh are not connected by railway route.

Suggestions

The following are some of the suggestions for the improvement of road system:

1. The Government should design a definite financial policy for the improvement of road sector. Sufficient amount of fund should be earmarked for the construction and maintenance of roads.

2. Considering the poor condition of existing road network, steps be taken for proper maintenance of the existing roads within the shortest possible time. The government should earmark definite fund for proper maintenance of existing road network;
3. Steps to be taken for technical of the road transport sector of the country. The means of road transport such as motor vehicle, trucks, bus, cars, etc. should adopt fuel efficient technology through technical improvement leading to fall in the unit cost of road transport;
4. The State Transport Corporation should be made autonomous so that they can manage their affairs freely without any interference from the Government. The activities of the corporation should be managed on profit oriented bases;
5. Considering the present requirement, private sector participation in the road sector on Build, Operated and Transfer (BOT) bases should be encouraged.

REFERENCES

1. Khan, R.R. Transport Management, *Himalaya Publishing House*, Bombay, 1980.
2. Jain, J.K. Transport Economics, *Chaitanya Publishing House*, Ahmedabad, 1987.
3. Dhar, P.K. Indian Economy, *Kalyani Publishers*, New Delhi, 2005.
4. *Economic Survey*, Government of Orissa, Bhubaneswar, 2004-05.
5. *Statistical Abstracts of Orissa*, Bhubaneswar, 2005.
6. *Districts at a Glance, Orissa*, Bhubaneswar, 2005.
7. *Report of the National Transport Policy Committee*, Chapter 1 and 2, 2005.

Index

A

Activities of OSTRC from the period 1992-93 to 2003-04, 89

Agriculture, 25

B

Behera, Chandra Sarat, 19

Brahma, K. Pradip, 54

British rule, 19, 20

C

Chhotroy, P.K., 8

D

Development of roads, 18-31

E

East India Company, 20

F

Financial analysis of ORT Co. Ltd. (1978-79 to 1989-90), 88

Freight traffic, 10

G

Gajapati district
- Bishoyis, 20, 21
- British rule, 19, 20
- development of roads, 18-31
- flora of Mahendragiri, 19
- forest roads, 27
- Ganjam agency, 19
- *Ganjam agency–population*, 27
- grand military road, 26
- *inam* lands, 21
- land revenue, 20
- list of *Muthas*, 21-31
- Madras Forest Act of 1882, 23
- major district road, 26
- Maliahs, 19, 20
- *mamools*, 25
- Muthas, 21
- Nandava forest, 19
- network, 23
- Parlakhemundi Zamindary, 20
- permanent settlement, 23
- rebels, 20
- reservation of vacancies, 25
- road communication, 26
- roads, 22
- sarvans, 23
- Taptapani ghat, 26
- tribal looks, 23
- village roads, 26

Goa, 10

H

I

India vision of rural road development, 11

Indian Railways, 51

Internal rail linkages, 40

K

Kerela, 10

L

Length of Indian roads, 50

M

Management of surface transport in India, 48-53
 introduction, 48-50
Market infrastructure, 8
Misra, Kumar Rookesh, 32
Misra, N.R., 32, 48
Misra, Narayana Rabi, 65, 81, 105
Mitra, Debabrata, 1
Modernization of the Railway system, 51
Mohanty, Chandra Prafulla, 92
Motor Vehicles Act, 1988, 5

N

Nagawali, 18
National Highway Authority of India, 39
Nayak, Sekhar Sudhansu, 81, 105
Network of supporting activities, 13
North Bengal State Transport Corporation, 1

O

Orissa, 18, 39, 54-64, 81-91, 92-104, 105-112
Own Your Wagon Schemes, 52

P

Panchayat Samiti roads, 69-70
Panda, Bharata, 18
Parlakimidi Rebellion, 20
Pattanayak, Pradeep Dr., 37
Peninsular India, 25
Phulbani district, 37
Pradhan Mantri Gram Sadak Yojana (PMGSY), 32, 76-79
Pradhan, Kumar Santosh, 65
Public sector undertaking, 81-91
Punjab, 9, 10

R

Railway bonds, 52
Railway transportation, 92-104
 analysis of the study, 93-98
 introduction, 92-93
 present position, 98-103
Railways, 9
Rajguru, S.N., 19
Rakesh Mohan Committee, 38
Raw materials, 49, 51
Road transport system, 105-112
 analysis, 111
 introduction, 105-106
 road network of central government, 107-110
 scope and objectives, 106-107
Road transport undertakings
 control of management for
  minimizing operating cost, 4-5
  cost on spares and assemblies, 5
  fuel cost, 5
  staff cost, 5
  tyre cost, 5
 – – – on cost of operations, 4
  minimizing operating costs, 4
  route economics, 4
 – – – related to utilisation of
  resources, 3
  government in business, 3

optimal utilisation of its main assets, 3-4
optimal utilisation of crew, 4
improved quality of public transport services, 5-6
introduction, 1-3
management control, 1-7
Role of surface transport for rural development, 8-17
gap in rural transportation demand and accessibility, 11
innovative technology for rural roads, 12
Pradhan Mantri Gram Sadak Yojana, 12
roads lead to economic prosperity, 8-9
rural connectivity, 10-11
status of transport infrastructure, 9-10
vision for rural development, 11-12
Role of surface transport in rural development, 37-47
demographic profile of Orissa, 39-40
– – – Phulbani, 41-43
rail transport, 51-52
road transport service in Orissa, 40-41
– – – – India, 39
– transportation, 50-51
– transport services in Phulbani district, 44-45
Role of transport in public sector undertaking of Orissa, 81-91
about the road transport, 82-83
about OSRTC, 87
analysis, 87-90
brief profile of ORT Co. Ltd., 85-86
introduction, 81-82
management of the company, 86
operational territory of the company, 86-87
scope and objectives, 82
transport development during plans in Orissa, 83-85
Rural India, 65
Rural road, 65-71
introduction, 65
key-indicator for rural development, 66-67
Panchayat Samiti roads of Aska Block, 69-70
road network in India, 66
rural road scenario of Orissa, 67
study of relevant, 67-69
Rusikulya, 18

S

Sahu, Kumar Anil, 48, 105
SAMUDRAM of costal Orissa, 13
Self-sufficient village economy, 13
Sharma, P.R., 54
Surface transport for rural development, 72-80
cost effective technology, 79
Indian scenario, 73
maintenance of rural roads, 79-80
Pradhan Mantri Gram Sadak Yojana, 76-79
present status of rural road connectivity, 74-75
rural road set-up, 74
significance of rural transport,

72-73
user responsiveness and peoples participation, 80
Surface transport in Orissa, 32-36
categories of vehicles, 35
motor vehicles position of the state, 34-36
national highways of the state, 33-34
rail transport, 36
roads in the state of Orissa, 33

T

Tekkali inscription, 19
Tempo-taxies, 9
Transport and economic development, 54-64
car and other four-wheelers, 59-61
composition of motor vehicles, 57-58
two-wheelers, 57
goods vehicles, 57
desity of motor vehicles, 55
economic development, 62-63
growth of motor vehicles, 55
– – vehicles in Orissa, 56
inter-state comparison, 55-57
network of roads, 61-62
Orissa scenario, 55
motor vehicles, 62-63
passenger buses, 58-59
share of road transport, 55
Transport infrastructure, 10
Transportation-infrastructure, 49
Tribals of Ganjam, 24
Trucks, 9

U

Uttar Pradesh, 9

V

Village connectivity with population 1000-1500, 15
Village connectivity with population less than 1000, 14

W

World Bank, 8

Z

Zamindars, 20, 23
Zamindary, 20

❑❑❑